Spurgeon's Sermons
on the
Cross
of Christ

C. H. Spurgeon Resources

Commenting and Commentaries
Day by Day with C. H. Spurgeon (compiled by Al Bryant)
The Treasury of David (edited by David Otis Fuller)
Spurgeon's Sermon Illustrations
Spurgeon's Sermon Notes
Spurgeon's Sermons on Angels
Spurgeon's Sermons for Christmas and Easter
Spurgeon's Sermons on the Cross of Christ
Spurgeon's Sermons on Family and Home
Spurgeon's Sermons on New Testament Miracles
Spurgeon's Sermons on Old Testament Men • Book One
Spurgeon's Sermons on Old Testament Men • Book Two
Spurgeon's Sermons on Old Testament Women • Book One
Spurgeon's Sermons on Old Testament Women • Book Two
Spurgeon's Sermons on New Testament Men • Book One
Spurgeon's Sermons on New Testament Men • Book Two
Spurgeon's Sermons on New Testament Women • Book One
Spurgeon's Sermons on New Testament Women • Book Two
Spurgeon's Sermons on the Parables of Christ
Spurgeon's Sermons on Great Prayers of the Bible
Spurgeon's Sermons on the Resurrection of Christ
Spurgeon's Sermons on Soulwinning
Spurgeon's Sermons on Special Days and Occasions

Spurgeon's Sermons
on the
Cross
of Christ

CHARLES HADDON SPURGEON

kregel
PUBLICATIONS

Grand Rapids, MI 49501

Spurgeon's Sermons on the Cross of Christ by Charles H. Spurgeon.

Copyright © 1993 by Kregel Publications.

Published in 1993 by Kregel Publications, a division of Kregel, Inc., P.O. Box 2607, Grand Rapids, MI 49501.

Cover and book design: Alan G. Hartman

Library of Congress Cataloging-in-Publication Data

Spurgeon, C. H. (Charles Haddon), 1834-1892.
   [Sermons on the cross of Christ]
   Spurgeon's Sermons on the cross of Christ / by Charles H. Spurgeon.
      p.   cm.
   1. Jesus Christ—Crucifixion—Sermons. 2. Sermons, English. I. Title.
BT450.S68   1993   232.96'3—dc20   93-13811
                                       CIP

ISBN 0-8254-3687-7 (pbk.)

2 3 4 5 printing / year 97 96

Printed in the United States of America

Contents

Foreword

The historicity of the crucifixion of Jesus underlies the entire New Testament and is even predicted in the Old Testament (i.e., Ps. 22). At its primary level, the crucifixion of Jesus was the means by which God provided salvation, the forgiveness of sins (see 1 Cor. 15:3). In fact, Christ crucified becomes the summary or summation of the Christian message. The Cross of Christ is the supreme demonstration of God's love for sinful man. This is the theme of the sermons selected for this compilation.

In his book, *The Crises of the Christ* (Kregel, 1989), Dr. G. Campbell Morgan points out the centrality of the Cross to our Christian faith:

> In that Cross . . . there is revealed the unclouded wisdom of God. Seeing all that man in his blindness failed to see, and knowing perfectly the whole fact of the depravity wrought by man, He yet originated and carried out a plan of redemption so wonderful that the very unfallen intelligences of the upper world have ever desired to look into this great mystery of wisdom, and no man has been able perfectly to fathom its depths. To the Jews a stumbling-block, something in the way over which they fall; to the Greeks utter foolishness; and yet blessed be God, both to Jew and Greek, not only power, but wisdom. What wondrous words were those that passed the lips of Jesus. "It is finished." What is finished? Sin was finished as to its power to work the final ruin of any man. In the mystery of the passion of Jesus, sin which had mastered men, and held them in slavery, was in turn mastered and robbed of its force. Whatever bruised, broken, beaten slave of sin will but hide in the cleft of that rock, and trust in the Crucified, for such an one sin is no more master. To the truth of this statement, testimony can be borne by the great multitudes of men and women who, standing at the Cross, have said, and still can say, The impossible has become possible, for all the forces of sin have been broken by the way of this victory of grace. Sin as a force that ruins, is ended in the Cross. It is not ended anywhere else. If men will not come into relation with that Cross, then sin is still an element of force, so great

that no man is equal to its overcoming. In the cleft rock there is perfect security and perfect victory. "It is finished," said the Master, and because He meant that sin was finished, He meant that the work was finished through which grace might flow out like a river.

So pivotal is a comprehension of the significance of the Cross to our Christian faith that this theme was one of the first selected for Kregel's multi-volume set of the "C. H. Spurgeon Sermon Series." It is a theme that underlies scores of the sermons scanned in preparation for this volume. May our Father bless these sermons to your heart and to your ministry.

AL BRYANT

Grand Rapids, Michigan
1993

1
*The Crown of Thorns** *

*And when they had platted a crown of thorns, they put it upon his
head (Matthew 27:29).*

Before we enter the common hall of the soldiers, and gaze upon "the sacred head once wounded," it will be well to consider who and what He was who was thus cruelly put to shame. Do not forget the intrinsic excellence of His person; for He is the brightness of the Father's glory, and the express image of His person; He is in Himself God over all, blessed forever, the eternal Word by whom all things were made, and by whom all things consist. Though Heir of all things, the Prince of the kings of the earth, He was despised and rejected of men, "a man of sorrows and acquainted with grief"; His head was scornfully surrounded with thorns for a crown, His body was bedecked with a faded purple robe, a poor reed was put into His hand for a scepter, and then the ribald soldiery dared to stare into His face, and worry Him with their filthy jests—

> The soldiers also spit upon that face
> Which angels did desire to have the grace,
> And prophets once to see, but found no place.
> Was ever grief like mine?

Do not forget the glory to which He had been accustomed aforetime, for before He came to earth He had been in the bosom of the Father, adored of cherubim and seraphim, obeyed by every angel, worshiped by every principality and power in the heavenly places; yet here He sits, treated worse than a felon, made the center of a comedy before He became the victim of a tragedy. They sat Him down in some broken chair, covered Him with an old soldier's cloak, and then insulted Him as a mimic monarch—

*   This sermon was preached on Sunday morning, April 13, 1874, and is taken from *The Metropolitan Tabernacle Pulpit*.

9

They bow their knees to me, and cry, Hail king;
Whatever scoffs and scornfulness can bring,
I am the floor, the sink, where they'd fling.
Was ever grief like mine?

What a descent His love to us compelled Him to make! See how low He fell to lift us from our fall! Do not also fail to remember that at the very time when they were thus mocking Him, He was still the Lord of all, and could have summoned twelve legions of angels to His rescue. There was majesty in His misery; He had laid aside, it is true, the glorious pomp imperial of His Father's courts, and He was now the lowly man of Nazareth, but for all that, had He willed it, one glance of those eyes would have withered up the Roman cohorts; one word from those silent lips would have shaken Pilate's palace from roof to foundation; and had He willed it, the vacillating governor and the malicious crowd would together have gone down alive into the pit, even as Korah, Dathan, and Abiram of old.

Lo, God's own Son, heaven's Darling, and earth's Prince, sits there and wears the cruel chaplet which wounds both mind and body at once, the mind with insult, and the body with piercing smart. His royal face was marred with "wounds which could not cease to bleed, trickling faint and slow," yet that "noblest brow and dearest" had once been fairer than the children of men, and was even then the countenance of Immanuel, God with us.

Remember these things, and you will gaze upon Him with enlightened eyes and tender hearts, and you will be able the more fully to enter into fellowship with Him in His griefs. Remember from whence He came, and it will the more astound you that He should have stooped so low. Remember what He was, and it will be the more marvelous that He should become our substitute.

And now let us press into the guardroom, and look at our Savior wearing His crown of thorns. I will not detain you long with any guesses as to what kind of thorns He wore. According to the Rabbis and the botanists there would seem to have been from twenty to twenty-five different species of thorny plants growing in Palestine; and different writers have, according to their own judgments or fancies, selected one and another of these plants as the peculiar thorns which were used upon this occasion. But why select one thorn out of many? He bore not one grief, but all; any and every thorn will suffice; the very dubiousness as to the peculiar species yields us instruction. It may well be that more than one kind of thorn was platted in that crown: at any rate sin has so thickly strewn the earth with thorns and thistles that there was no difficulty in finding the materials, even as there was no scarcity of griefs with which to chasten Him every morning and make Him a mourner all His days.

The soldiers may have used pliant boughs of the acacia, or shittim tree, that unrotting wood of which many of the sacred tables and vessels of the sanctuary were made; and, therefore, significantly used if such was the case. It may have been true, as the old writers generally consider, that the plant was the *spina Christi*, for it has many small and sharp spines, and its green leaves would have made a wreath such as those with which generals and emperors were crowned after a battle. But we will leave the matter; it was a crown of thorns which pierced His head, and caused Him suffering as well as shame, and that suffices us. Our inquiry now is, what do we see when our eyes behold Jesus Christ crowned with thorns? There are six things which strike me most, and as I lift the curtain I pray you watch with me, and may the Holy Spirit pour forth His divine illumination and light up the scene before our wondering souls.

A Sorrowful Spectacle

The first thing which is seen by the most casual observer, before He looks beneath the surface, is a SORROWFUL SPECTACLE. Here is the Christ, the generous, loving, tender Christ, treated with indignity and scorn; here is the Prince of Life and Glory made an object of derision by a ribald soldiery. Behold today the lily among thorns, purity lifting up itself in the midst of opposing sin. See here the sacrifice caught in the thicket, and held fast there, as a victim in our stead to fulfill the ancient type of the ram held by the bushes, which Abraham slew instead of Isaac. Three things are to be carefully noted in this spectacle of sorrow.

Here is Christ's *lowliness and weakness triumphed over* by the lusty legionaries. When they brought Jesus into the guardroom they felt that He was entirely in their power, and that His claim to be a king were so absurd as to be only a theme for contemptuous jest. He was but meanly dressed, for He wore only the smock frock of a peasant—was He a claimant of the purple? He held His peace—was He the man to stir a nation to sedition? He was all wounds and bruises, fresh from the scourger's lash—was He the hero to inspire an army's enthusiasm and overturn old Rome? It seemed rare mirth for them, and as wild beasts sport with their victims, so did they. Many, I warrant you, were the jibes and jeers of the Roman soldiery at His expense, and loud was the laughter amid their ranks.

Look at His face, how meek He appears! How different from the haughty countenances of tyrants! To mock His royal claims seemed but natural to a rough soldiery. He was gentle as a child, tender as a woman; His dignity was that of calm quiet endurance, and this was not a dignity whose force these semibarbarous men could feel, therefore did they pour contempt upon Him.

Let us remember that our Lord's weakness was undertaken for our sakes: for us He became a lamb, for us He laid aside His glory, and therefore it is the more painful for us to see that this voluntary humiliation of

Himself must be made the object of so much derision and scorn, though worthy of the utmost praise. He stoops to save us, and we laugh at Him as He stoops; He leaves the throne that He may lift us up to it, but while He is graciously descending, the hoarse laughter of an ungodly world is His only reward. Ah me! was ever love treated after so unlovely a sort? Surely the cruelty it received was proportioned to the honor it deserved, so perverse are the sons of men.

> O head so full of bruises!
> Brown that its lifeblood loses!
> O great humility.
> Upon His face are falling
> Indignities most galling;
> He bears them all for me.

It was not merely that they mocked His humility, but *they mocked His claims to be a king.* "Aha," they seemed to say, "is this a king? It must be after some uncouth Jewish fashion, surely, that this poor peasant claims to wear a crown. Is this the Son of David? When will He drive Cæsar and his armies into the sea, and set up a new state, and reign at Rome? This Jew, this peasant, is He to fulfill His nation's dream, and rule over all mankind?"

Wonderfully did they ridicule this idea, and we do not wonder that they did, for they could not perceive His true glory. But, beloved, my point lies here, *He was a King* in the truest and most emphatic sense. If He had not been a king, then He would as an impostor have deserved the scorn, but would not have keenly felt it; but being truly and really a king, every word must have stung His royal soul, and every syllable must have cut to the quick His kingly spirit. When the impostor's claims are exposed and held up to scorn, he himself must well know that he deserves all the contempt he receives, and what can he say? But if the real heir to all the estates of heaven and earth has His claims denied and His person mocked at, then is His heart wounded, and rebuke and reproach fill Him with many sorrows. Is it not sad that the Son of God, the blessed and only Potentate, should have been thus disgraced?

Nor was it merely mockery, but *cruelty added pain to insult.* If they had only intended to mock Him they might have platted a crown of straw, but they meant to pain Him, and therefore they fashioned a crown of thorns. Look, I pray you, at His person as He suffers under their hands. They had scourged Him till probably there was no part of His body which was not bleeding beneath their blows except His head, and now that head must be made to suffer too. Alas, our whole head was sick, and our whole heart faint, and so He must be made in His chastisement like to us in our transgression. There was no part of our humanity without sin, and there must be no part of His humanity without suffering.

If we had escaped in some measure from iniquity, so might He have escaped from pain, but as we had worn the foul garment of transgression, and it covered us from head to foot, even so must He wear the garments of shame and derision from the crown of His head even to the sole of His foot.

> O Love, too boundless to be shown
> By any but the Lord alone!
> O Love offended, which sustains
> The bold offender's curse and pains!
> O Love, which could no motive have,
> But mere benignity to save.

Beloved, I always feel as if my tongue were tied when I come to talk of the sufferings of my Master. I can think of them, I can picture them to myself, I can sit down and weep over them, but I do not know how to paint them to others. Did you ever know pen or pencil that could? A Michael Angelo or a Raphael might well shrink back from attempting to paint this picture; and the tongue of an archangel might be consumed in the effort to sing the griefs of Him who was loaded with shame because of our shameful transgressions. I ask you rather to meditate than to listen, and to sit down and view your Lord with your own loving eyes rather than to have regard to words of mine. I can only sketch the picture, roughly outlining it as with charcoal; I must leave you to put into the colors, and then to sit and study it, but you will fail as I do. Dive we may, but we cannot reach the depths of this abyss of woe and shame. Mount we may, but these storm-swept hills of agony are still above us.

A Solemn Warning

Removing the curtain again from this sorrowful spectacle, I see here a SOLEMN WARNING which speaks softly and meltingly to us out of the spectacle of sorrow. Do you ask me what is that warning? It is a warning against our ever committing the same crime as the soldiers did. "The same!" say you; "why, we should never plat a crown of thorns for that dear head." I pray you never may; but there are many who have done, and are doing it.

They are guilty of this crime who, as these soldiers did, *deny His claims*. Busy are the wise men of this world at this very time all over the world, busy in gathering thorns and twisting them, that they may afflict the Lord's Anointed. Some of them cry, "Yes, He was a good man, but not the Son of God"; others even deny His superlative excellence in life and teaching; they cavil at His perfection, and imagine flaws where none exist. Never are they happier than when impugning His character.

I may be addressing some avowed infidel here, some skeptic as to the Redeemer's person and doctrine, and I charge him with crowning the

Christ of God with thorns every time he invents bitter charges against the Lord Jesus, and utters railing words against His cause and His people. Your denial of His claims, and especially your ridicule of them, is a repetition of the unhappy scene before us. There are some who ply all their wit, and tax their utmost skill for nothing else but to discover discrepancies in the gospel narratives, or to conjure up differences between their supposed scientific discoveries and the declarations of the Word of God. Full often have they torn their own hands in weaving crowns of thorns when they come to die, as the result of their displays of scientific research after briers with which to afflict the Lover of mankind.

It will be well if they have not to lie on worse than thorns forever, when Christ shall come to judge them and condemn them and cast them into the lake of fire for all their impieties concerning Him. O that they would cease this useless and malicious trade of weaving crowns of thorns for Him who is the world's only hope, whose religion is the lone star that gilds the midnight of human sorrow, and guides mortal man to the port of peace! Even for the temporal benefits of Christianity the good Jesus should be treated with respect; He has emancipated the slave, and uplifted the down-trodden; His gospel is the charter of liberty, the scourge of freedom, order, love, and joy. He is the greatest of philanthropists, the truest friend of man, wherefore then array yourselves against Him, you who talk of progress and enlightenment? If men did but know Him they would crown Him with diadems of reverent love, more precious than the pearls of India for His reign will usher in the golden age, and even now it softens the rigor of the present, as it has removed the miseries of the past. It is an ill business, this carping and caviling, and I beseech those engaged in it to cease their ungenerous labors, worthy of rational beings and destructive to their immortal souls.

This crowning with thorns is wrought in another fashion by *hypocritical professions of allegiance to Him.* These soldiers put a crown on Christ's head, but they did not mean that He should be king; they put a scepter in His hand, but it was not the substantial ivory rod which signifies real power, it was only a weak and slender reed. Therein they remind us that Christ is mocked by insincere professors. O you who love Him not in your inmost souls, you are those who mock Him: but you say, "Wherein have I failed to crown Him? Did I not join the church? Have I not said that I am a believer?" But if your hearts are not right within you, you have only crowned Him with thorns; if you have not given Him your very soul, you have in awful mockery thrust a scepter of reed into His hand.

Your very religion mocks Him. Your lying professions mock Him. Who has required this at your hands, to tread His courts? You insult Him at His table! You insult Him on your knees! How can you say you love Him, when your hearts are not with Him? If you have never believed in Him and repented of sin, and yielded obedience to His command, if you do not own Him in your daily life to be both Lord and King, I charge you lay down the profession which is so dishonoring to Him.

If He be God, serve Him; if He be King, obey Him; if He be neither, then do not profess to be Christians. Be honest and bring no crown if you do not accept Him as King. What need again to insult Him with nominal dominion, mimic homage, and pretended service? O hypocrites, consider your ways, lest soon the Lord whom you provoke should ease Him of His adversaries.

In a measure the same thing may be done by those who are sincere, but through want of watchfulness *walk so as to dishonor their profession.* Here, if I speak rightly, I shall compel every one of you to confess it in your spirits that you stand condemned; for every time that we act according to our sinful flesh we crown the Savior's head with thorns. Which of us has not done this? Dear head, every hair of which is more precious than fine gold, when we gave our hearts to you we thought we should always adore you, that our whole lives would be one long psalm, praising and blessing and crowning you. Alas, how far have we fallen short of our own ideal! We have hedged you about with the briers of our sin. We have been betrayed into angry tempers, so that we have spoken unadvisedly with our lips; or we have been worldly, and loved that which you abhor, or we have yielded to our passions, and indulged our evil desires. Our vanities, follies, forgetfulnesses, omissions, and offenses have set upon your head a coronet of dishonor, and we tremble to think of it.

O cruel hearts and hands to have so maltreated the Well-beloved, whom it should have been our daily care to glorify! Do I speak to any backslider whose open sin has dishonored the cross of Christ? I fear I must be addressing some who once had a name to live, but now are numbered with the dead in sin. Surely if there be a spark of grace in you, what I am now saying must cut you to the quick, and act like salt upon a raw wound to make your very soul to smart. Do not your ears tingle as I accuse you deliberately of acts of inconsistency which have twisted a thorny crown for our dear Master's head? It is assuredly so, for you have opened the mouths of blasphemers, taught gainsayers to revile Him, grieved the generation of His people, and made many to stumble. Ungodly men have laid your faults at the door of the innocent Savior; they have said, "This is your religion."

You have grown the thorns, but He has had to wear them. *We* call our offenses inconsistencies, but worldly men regard them as the fruit of Christianity, and condemn the vine because of our sour clusters. They charge the holy Jesus with the faults of His erring followers. Dear friends, is there not room to look at home in the case of each one of us? As we do so, let us come with the sorrowful and loving penitent, and wash His dear feet with tears of repentance, because we have crowned His head with thorns.

Thus our thorn-crowned Lord and Master stands before us as a sorrowful spectacle, conveying to us a solemn warning.

Triumphant Endurance

Lifting the veil again, in the person of our tortured and insulted Lord we see TRIUMPHANT ENDURANCE. He could not be conquered, He was victorious even in the hour of deepest shame.

> He with unflinching heart
> Bore all disgrace and shame,
> And 'mid the keenest smart
> Lov'd on, yea lov'd the same.

He was bearing at the moment, first, *the substitutionary griefs* which were due to Him because He stood in our place, and from bearing them He did not turn aside. We were sinners, and the reward of sin is pain and death, therefore He bore the chastisement of our peace. He was enduring at that time what we ought to have endured, and draining the cup which justice had mingled for us. Did He start back from it? O, no. When first He came to drink of that wormwood and gall in the garden He put it to His lips, and the draught seemed for an instant to stagger His strong spirit. His soul was exceeding sorrowful, even unto death. He was like one demented, tossed to and fro with inward agony. "My Father," said He, "if it be possible, let this cup pass from me." Thrice did He utter that prayer, while every portion of His manhood was the battlefield of legions of griefs. His soul rushed out at every pore to find a vent for its swelling woes, His whole body being covered with gory sweat.

After that tremendous struggle the strength of love mastered the weakness of manhood; He put that cup to His lips and never shrank, but He drank right on till not a dreg was left; and now the cup of wrath is empty, no trace of the terrible wine of the wrath of God can be found within it. At one tremendous draught of love the Lord forever drank destruction dry for all His people. "Who is he that condemneth? It is Christ that died, yea, rather, that hath risen again," and "there is therefore now no condemnation to them that are in Christ Jesus, who walk not after the flesh but after the Spirit."

Now surely endurance had reached a very high point when He was made to endure the painful mockery which our text describes, yet He quailed not, nor removed from His settled purpose. He had undertaken, and He would go through with it. Look at Him, and see there a miracle of patient endurance of griefs which would have sent a world to hell had He not borne them on our behalf.

Besides the shame and suffering due for sin, with which it pleased the Father to bruise Him, He was enduring *overwhelming malice from the hate of men.* Why did men have to concentrate all their scorn and cruelty into His execution? Was it not enough that He must die? Did it give pleasure to their iron hearts to rack His tenderest sensibilities? Wherefore these inventions for deepening His woe? Had any of us been thus derided we should have resented it. There is not a man or woman here who could have been silent under such indignities, but Jesus sat in omnipotence of patience, possessing His soul right royally. Glorious pattern of patience, we adore You as we see how malice could not conquer Your almighty love!

The pain which He had endured from the scourges caused Him to throb with exquisite anguish, but we read neither of tears nor groans, much less of angry complaints or revengeful threats. He does not seek for pity, or make one appeal for lenity. He does not ask why they torture or why they mock.

Brave witness! Courageous martyr! Suffering exquisitely You also suffer calmly. Such a perfect frame as His, His body being conceived without sin, must have been capable of tortures which our bodies, unstrung by sin, cannot feel. His delicate purity felt a horror of ribald jests which our more hardened spirits cannot estimate, yet Jesus bore all, as only the Son of God could bear it. They might heap on the load as they would, He would only put forth more endurance, and bear it all, but shrink or quail He would not.

I venture to suggest that such was the picture of patience which our blessed Lord exhibited that it may have moved some even of the soldiery themselves. Has it ever occurred to you to ask how Matthew came to know all about that mockery? Matthew was not there. Mark also gives an account of it, but he would not have been tolerated in the guardroom. The Praetorians were far too proud and rough to tolerate Jews, much less disciples of Jesus, in their common hall. Since there could have been nobody there except the legionaries themselves, it is well to inquire—Who told this tale?

It must have been an eyewitness. May it not have been that centurion who in the same chapter is reported to have said, "Certainly this was the Son of God"? May not that scene as well as the Lord's death have led him to that conclusion? We do not know, but this much is very evident, the story must have been told by an eyewitness, and also by one who sympathized with the sufferer, for to my ear it does not read like the description of an unconcerned spectator. I should not wonder—I would almost venture to assert—that our Lord's marred but patient visage preached such a sermon that one at least who gazed upon it felt its mysterious power, felt that such patience was more than human, and accepted the thorn-crowned Savior as henceforth his Lord and his King. This I do know, that if you and I want to conquer human hearts for Jesus we must be patient too; and if, when they ridicule and persecute us, we can but endure without repining or retaliation, we shall exercise an influence which even the most brutal will feel, and to which chosen minds will submit themselves.

A Sacred Medicine

Drawing up the veil again, I think we have before us, in the fourth place, in the person of the triumphant sufferer, a SACRED MEDICINE. I can only hint at the diseases which it will cure. These blood-besprinkled thorns are plants of renown, precious in heavenly surgery if they be rightly used. Take but a thorn out of this crown and use it as a lancet, and it will let out the hot blood of passion and abate the fever of pride; it is a wonderful remedy for swelling flesh and grievous boils of sin. He who sees Jesus crowned with thorns will loathe to look on self, except it be through tears of contrition. This thorn at the breast will make men sing, but not with notes of self-congratulation, the notes will be those of a dove moaning for her mate.

Gideon taught the men of Succoth with thorns, but the lessons were not so salutary as those which we learn from the thorns of Jesus. The sacred medicine which the good Physician brings to us in His thorny chaplet acts as a tonic, and strengthens us to endure without depression whatever shame or loss His service may bring upon us:

> Who defeats my fiercest foes?
> Who consoles my saddest woes?
> Who revives my fainting heart,
> Healing all its hidden smart?
> Jesus crowned with thorns.

When you begin to serve God, and for His sake endeavor to benefit your fellow-mortals, do not expect any reward from men, except to be misunderstood, suspected, and abused. The best men in the world are usually the worst spoken of. An evil world cannot speak well of holy lives. The sweetest fruit is most pecked at by the birds, the most heaven-nearing mountain is most beaten by the storms, and the loveliest character is the most assailed. Those whom you would save will not thank you for your anxiety, but blame you for your interference. If you rebuke their sins they will frequently resent your warnings, if you invite them to Jesus, they will make light of your entreaties. Are you prepared for this? If not, consider Him who endured such contradiction of sinners against Himself lest you be weary and faint in your minds.

If you succeed in bringing many to Christ, you must not reckon upon universal honor. Rather, you will be charged with self-seeking, popularity-hunting, or some such crime; you will be misrepresented, belied, caricatured, and counted as a fool or a knave by the ungodly world. The probabilities are that the crown you will win in this world, if you serve God, will contain more spikes than sapphires, more briers than berlys.

When it is put upon your head pray for grace to wear it right gladly, counting it all joy to be like your Lord. Say in your heart, "I feel no dishonor in this dishonor. Men may impute shameful things to me, but I am not ashamed. They may degrade me, but I am not degraded. They may cast contempt upon me, but I am not contemptible." The Master of the house was called Beelzebub and spit upon; they cannot do worse to his household, therefore we scorn their scorn. Thus are we nerved to patience by the patience of the despised Nazarene.

The thorn crown is also a remedy for discontent and affliction. When enduring bodily pain we are apt to wince and fret, but if we remember Jesus crowned with thorns, we say—

> His way was much rougher and darker than mine;
> Did Christ my Lord suffer, and shall I repine?

And so our complaints grow dumb; for very shame we dare not compare our maladies with His woes. Resignation is learned at Jesus' feet, when we see our great Exemplary made perfect through suffering.

The thorn crown is a cure for care. We would cheerfully wear any array which our Lord may prepare for us, but it is a great folly to plat hope, true believers take much trouble to trouble themselves, and labor to increase their own labor. They haste to be rich, they fret, they toil, they worry, and torment themselves to load themselves with the burden of wealth; they wound themselves to wear the thorny crown of worldly greatness.

Many are the ways of making rods for our own backs. I have known mothers to make thorn crowns out of their children whom they could not trust with God; they have been worn with family anxieties when they might have rejoiced in God. I have known others to make thorn crowns out of silly fears, for which there were no grounds whatever; but they seemed ambitious to be fretful, eager to prick themselves with briers. O believer, say to yourself, "My Lord wore my crown of thorns for me; why should I wear it too?" He took our griefs and carried our sorrows that we might be a happy people, and be able to obey the command, "Take no thought for the morrow, for the morrow shall take thought for the things of itself." Ours is the crown of loving kindness and tender mercies, and we wear it when we cast all our care on Him who cares for us.

That thorn crown cures us of desire for the vainglories of the world. It dims all human pomp and glory till it turns to smoke. Could we fetch hither the Pope's triple crown, or the imperial diadem of Germany, or the regalia of the Czar of All the Russias, what of them all compared with Jesus' crown of thorns? Let us set some great one on his throne, and see how little he looks when Jesus sits beside him. What is there kingly in being able to tax men, and live upon their labors, giving little in return? The royalest thing is to lay them all under obligations to our disinterested love, and be the fountain of blessing to them. O, it takes the glitter from your gold, and the luster from your gems, and the beauty from all your dainty gewgaws, to see that no imperial purple can equal the glory of His blood, no gems can rival His thorns. Show and parade cease to attract the soul when once the superlative excellencies of the dying Savior have been discerned by the enlightened eye.

Who seeks for ease when he has seen the Lord Christ? If Christ wears a crown of thorns, shall we covet a crown of laurel? Even the fierce Crusader when he entered into Jerusalem, and was elected king, had sense enough to say, "I will not wear a crown of gold in the same city where my Savior wore a crown of thorns." Why should we desire, like feather-bed soldiers, to have everything arranged for our ease and pleasure? Why this reclining upon couches when Jesus hangs on a cross? Why this soft raiment when He is naked? Why these luxuries when He is barbarously entreated? Thus the thorn crown cures us at once of the vainglory of the world, and of our own selfish love of ease. The world's minstrel may cry, "Ho, boy, come hither, and crown me with rose buds!" but the voluptuary's request is not for us. For us neither delights of the flesh nor the pride of life can have charms while the Man of Sorrows is in view. For us it remains to suffer, and to labor, till the King shall bid us share His rest.

A Mystic Coronation

I must notice in the fifth place that there is before us a MYSTIC CORONATION. Bear with my many divisions. The coronation of Christ with thorns was symbolical, and had great meaning in it, for, first, it was to Him *a triumphal crown*. Christ had fought with sin from the day when He first stood foot to foot with it in the wilderness up to the time when He entered Pilate's hall, and He had conquered it. As a witness that He had gained the victory behold sin's crown seized as a trophy! What was the crown of sin? Thorns. These sprang from the curse. "Thorns also and thistles shall it bring forth to thee," was the coronation of sin, and now Christ has taken away its crown, and put it on His own head. He has spoiled sin of its richest regalia, and He wears it Himself. Glorious champion, all hail!

What if I say that the thorns constituted a mural crown? Paradise was set round with a hedge of thorns so sharp that none could enter it, but our champion leaped first upon the bristling rampart, and bore the blood-red banner of His crown into the heart of that better new Eden, which thus He won for us never to be lost again. Jesus wears the mural chaplet which denotes that He has opened Paradise. It was a wrestler's crown He wore, for He did not wrestle with flesh and blood, but with principalities and powers, and He overthrew His foe. It was a racer's crown He wore, for He had run with the mighty and outstripped them in the race. He had well-nigh finished His course, and had but a step or two more to take to reach the goal.

Here is a marvelous field for enlargement, and we must stay at once lest we go too far. It was a crown rich with glory, despite the shame which was intended by it. We see in Jesus the monarch of the realms of misery, the chief among ten thousand sufferers. Never say, "I am a great sufferer." What are our griefs compared with His? As the poet stood upon the Palatine Mount and thought of Rome's dire ruin, he exclaimed, "What are our woes and sufferings?" Even so I ask, What are our shallow griefs compared with the infinite sorrows of Immanuel? Well may we "control in our close breasts our petty misery."

Jesus is, moreover, the prince of martyrs. He leads the van among the noble army of suffering witnesses and confessors of the truth. Though they died at the stake, or pined in dungeons, or were cast to wild beasts, none of them claim the first rank; but He, the faithful and the true witness, with the thorn crown and the cross, stands at the head of them all. It may never be our lot to join the august band, but if there be an honor for which we might legitimately envy saints of former times, it is this, that they were born in those brave days when the ruby crown was within human grasp, and when the supreme sacrifice might have been made.

We are cravens, indeed, if in these softer days we are ashamed to confess our Master, and are afraid of a little scorn, or tremble at the criticisms of the would-be wise. Rather let us follow the Lamb whithersoever He goes, content to wear His crown of thorns that we may in His kingdom behold His glory.

A Mighty Stimulus

The last word is this. In the thorn crown I see a MIGHTY STIMULUS. A mighty stimulus to what? Why, first, to *fervent love of Him.* Can you see Him crowned with thorns and not be drawn to Him? If He could come among us this morning, and we could see Him, there would be a loving press around Him to touch the hem of His garment or to kiss His feet. Savior, You are very precious to us. Dearest of all the names above, my Savior and my God, You are always glorious. But in these eyes You are never more lovely than when arrayed in shameful mockery. The Lily of the Valley, and the Rose of Sharon, both in one is He, fair in the perfection of His character, and blood-red in the greatness of His sufferings. Worship Him! Adore Him! Bless Him! And let your voices sing, "Worthy is the Lamb."

This sight is a stimulus, next, to *repentance.* Did our sins put thorns around His head? O, my poor fallen nature, I will scourge you for scourging Him, and make you feel the thorns for causing Him to endure them. What, can you see your best Beloved put to such shame, and yet hold truce or parley with the sins which pierced Him? It cannot be. Let us declare before God our soul's keen grief that we should make the Savior suffer so;

then let us pray for grace to hedge our lives around with thorns that from this very day sin may not approach us.

I thought this day of how ofttimes I have seen the blackthorn growing in the hedge all bristling with a thousand prickles, but right in the center of the bush have I seen the pretty nest of a little bird. Why did the creature place its habitation there? Because the thorns become a protection to it, and shelter it from harm. As I meditated last night upon this blessed subject, I thought I would bid you build your nests within the thorns of Christ. It is a safe place for sinners. Neither Satan, sin, nor death can reach you there. Gaze on your Savior's sufferings, and you will see sin atoned for. Fly into His wounds! fly, you timid trembling doves! There is no resting-place so safe for you. Build your nests, I say again, among these thorns, and when you have done so, and trusted Jesus, and counted Him to be all in all to you, then come and crown His sacred head with other crowns.

What glory does He deserve? What is good enough for Him? If we could take all the precious things from all the treasuries of monarchs, they would not be worthy to be pebbles beneath His feet. If we could bring Him all the scepters, miters, tiaras, diadems, and all other pomp of earth, they would be altogether unworthy to be thrown in the dust before Him.

Wherewith shall we crown Him? Come let us weave our praises together and set our tears for pearls, our love for gold. They will sparkle like so many diamonds in His esteem, for He loves repentance, and He loves faith. Let us make a chaplet this morning with our praises, and crown Him as the laureate of grace. This day on which He rose from the dead, let us extol Him. O, for grace to do it in the heart, and then in the life, and then with the tongue, that we may praise Him forever who bowed His head to shame for us.

2
*Christ Made a Curse for Us**

Christ hath redeemed us from the curse of the law, being made a curse for us: for it is written, Cursed is every one that hangeth on a tree (Galatians 3:13).

The apostle had been showing to the Galatians that salvation is in no degree by works. He proved this all-important truth in the verses which precede the text, by a very conclusive form of double reasoning. He showed, first, that the law could not give the blessing of salvation, for, since all had broken it, all that the law could do was to curse. He quotes the substance of the twenty-seventh chapter of Deuteronomy, "Cursed is every one that continueth not in all things which are written in the book of the law to do them"; and as no man can claim that he has continued in all things that are in the law, he pointed out the clear inference that all men under the law had incurred the curse. He then reminds the Galatians, in the second place, that if any had ever been blessed in the old times, the blessing came not by the law, but by their faith, and to prove this, he quotes a passage from Habakkuk 2:4, in which it is distinctly stated that the just shall live by faith: so that those who were just and righteous, did not live before God on the basis of their obedience to the law, but they were justified and made to live on the ground of their being believers.

See, then, that if the law inevitably curses us all, and if the only people who are said to have been preserved in gracious life were justified not by works, but by faith, then is it certain beyond a doubt that the salvation and justification of a sinner cannot be by the works of the law, but altogether by the grace of God through faith which is in Christ Jesus. But the apostle, no doubt feeling that now he was declaring that doctrine, he had better declare the foundation and root of it, unveils in the text before us a reason why men are not saved by their personal righteousness, but saved by their faith. He tells us that the reason is this: that men are not saved now by any

*   This sermon was preached on Sunday morning, May 30, 1869, and is taken from *The Metropolitan Tabernacle Pulpit.*

personal merit, but their salvation lies in another—lies, in fact, in Christ Jesus, the representative Man, who alone can deliver us from the curse which the law brought upon us; and since works do not connect us with Christ, but faith is the uniting bond, faith becomes the way of salvation.

Since faith is the hand that lays hold upon the finished work of Christ, which works could not and would not do, for works lead us to boast and to forget Christ, faith becomes the true and only way of obtaining justification and everlasting life. In order that such faith may be nurtured in us, may God the Holy Spirit this morning lead us into the depths of the great work of Christ; may we understand more clearly the nature of His substitution, and of the suffering which it entailed upon Him. Let us see, indeed, the truth of the stanzas whose music has just died away—

> He bore that we might never bear
> His Father's righteous ire.

What Is the Curse of the Law Here Intended?

Our first contemplation will be upon this question: WHAT IS THE CURSE OF THE LAW HERE INTENDED? It is the curse of God. God who made the law has appended certain penal consequences to the breaking of it, and the man who violates the law becomes at once the subject of the wrath of the Lawgiver. It is not the curse of the mere law of itself; it is a curse from the great Lawgiver whose arm is strong to defend His statutes. Hence, at the very outset of our reflections, let us be assured that the law-curse must be supremely just, and morally unavoidable. It is not possible that our God, who delights to bless us, should inflict an atom of curse upon any one of His creatures unless the highest right shall require it; and if there be any method by which holiness and purity can be maintained without a curse, rest assured the God of love will not imprecate sorrow upon His creatures.

The curse then, if it fall, must be a necessary one, in its very essence needful for the preservation of order in the universe, and for the manifestation of the holiness of the universal Sovereign. Be assured, too, that when God curses, it is a curse of the most weighty kind. The curse causeless shall not come; but God's curses are never causeless, and they come home to offenders with overwhelming power. Sin must be punished, and when by long continuance and impenitence in evil, God is provoked to speak the malediction, I declare that he whom He curses, is cursed indeed. There is something so terrible in the very idea of the omnipotent God pronouncing a curse upon a transgressor, that my blood curdles at it, and I cannot express myself very clearly or even coherently.

A father's curse, how terrible! But what is that to the malediction of the great Father of Spirits! To be cursed of men is no mean evil, but to be accursed of God is terror and dismay. Sorrow and anguish lie in that curse;

death is involved in it and that second death which John foresaw in Patmos, and described as being cast into a lake of fire (Rev. 20:14). Hear the word of the Lord by His servant Nahum, and consider what His curse must be: "God is jealous, and the Lord revengeth; the Lord revengeth, and is furious; the Lord will take vengeance on his adversaries, and he reserveth wrath for his enemies. . . . The mountains quake at him, and the hills melt, and the earth is burned at his presence, yea, the world, and all that dwell herein. Who can stand before his indignation? and who can abide in the fierceness of his anger? his fury is poured out like fire, and the rocks are thrown down by him."

Remember also the prophecy of Malachi: "For behold, the day cometh, that shall burn as an oven; and all the proud, yea, and all that do wickedly, shall be stubble: and the day that cometh shall burn them up, saith the Lord of hosts, that it shall leave them neither root nor branch." Let such words, and there are many like them, sink into your hearts, that you may fear and tremble before this just and holy Lord.

If we would look further into the meaning of the curse that arises from the breach of the law, we must remember that a curse is first of all a sign of displeasure. Now, we learn from Scripture that God is angry with the wicked every day; though toward the persons of sinners God exhibits great longsuffering, yet sin exceedingly provokes His holy mind; sin is a thing so utterly loathsome and detestable to the purity of the Most High, that no thought of evil, nor an ill word, nor an unjust action, is tolerated by Him; He observes every sin, and His holy soul is stirred thereby. He is of purer eyes than to behold iniquity; He cannot endure it. He is a God who will certainly execute vengeance upon every evil work.

A curse implies something more than mere anger. It is suggested by burning indignation; and truly our God is not only somewhat angry with sinners, but His wrath is great toward sin. Wherever sin exists, there the fullness of the power of the divine indignation is directed; and though the effect of that wrath may be for awhile restrained through abundant longsuffering, yet God is greatly indignant with the iniquities of men. We wink at sin, yes, and even harden our hearts till we laugh at it and take pleasure in it, but oh! let us not think that God is such as we are; let us not suppose that sin can be beheld by Him and yet no indignation be felt. Ah! no, the most holy God has written warnings in His Word which plainly inform us how terribly He is provoked by iniquity, as, for instance, when He says, "Beware, ye that forget God, lest I tear you in pieces, and there be none to deliver." "Therefore saith the Lord, the Lord of hosts, the mighty One of Israel, Ah, I will ease me of mine adversaries, and avenge me of mine enemies." "For we know him that hath said, Vengeance belongeth unto me, I will recompense, saith the Lord. And again, the Lord shall judge His people. It is a fearful thing to fall into the hands of the living God."

Moreover, a curse imprecates evil, and is, as it comes from God, of the nature of a threat. It is as though God should say, "By-and-by I will visit you for this offense. You have broken My law which is just and holy, and the inevitable penalty shall certainly come upon you." Now, God has throughout His Word given many such curses as these; He has threatened men over and over again. "If he turn not, he will whet his sword; he hath bent his bow, and made it ready." Sometimes the threatening is wrapped up in a plaintive lamentation. "Turn ye, turn ye from your evil ways; for why will ye die, O house of Israel?" But still it is plain and clear that God will not allow sin to go unpunished, and when the fullness of time shall come, and the measure shall be filled to the brim, and the weight of iniquity shall be fully reached, and the harvest shall be ripe, and the cry of wickedness shall come up mightily into the ears of the Lord God of Sabaoth, then will He come forth in robes of vengeance and overwhelm His adversaries.

But God's curse is something more than a threatening; He comes at length to blows. He uses warning words at first, but sooner or later He bares His sword for execution. The curse of God, as to its actual infliction, may be guessed at by some occasions wherein it has been seen on earth. Look at Cain, a wanderer and a vagabond upon the face of the earth! Read the curse that Jeremiah pronounced by the command of God upon Pashur: "Behold, I will make thee a terror to thyself, and to all thy friends: and they shall fall by the sword of their enemies, and thine eyes shall behold it."

Or, if you would behold the curse upon a larger scale, remember the day when the huge floodgates of earth's deepest fountains were unloosed, and the waters leaped up from their habitations like lions eager for their prey. Remember the day of vengeance when the windows of heaven were opened, and the great deep above the firmament was confused with the deep that is beneath the firmament, and all flesh were swept away, save only the few who were hidden in the ark which God's covenant mercy had prepared—when sea-monsters whelped and stabled in the palaces of ancient kings, when millions of sinners sank to rise no more, when universal ruin flew with raven wing over a shoreless sea vomited from the mouth of death. Then was the curse of God poured out upon the earth.

Look yet again further down in time. Stand with Abraham at his tent door, and see toward the east the sky all red at early morning with a glare that came not from the sun; sheets of flames went up to heaven, which were met by showers of yet more vivid fire, which preternaturally descended from the skies. Sodom and Gomorrah, having given themselves up to strange flesh, received the curse of God, and hell was rained upon them out of heaven until they were utterly consumed.

If you would see another form of the curse of God, remember that bright spirit who once stood as servitor in heaven, the son of the morning, one of the chief of the angels of God. Think how he lost his lofty principality when sin entered into him! See how an archangel became an archfiend, and Satan, who is called Apollyon, fell from his lofty throne, banished forever from peace and happiness, to wander through dry places, seeking rest and finding none, to be reserved in chains of darkness unto the judgment of the last great day.

Such was the curse that it withered an angel into a devil, it burned up the cities of the plain, it swept away the population of a globe. Nor have you yet the full idea. There is a place of woe and horror, a land of darkness as darkness itself, and of the shadow of death, without any order, and where the light is darkness. There those miserable spirits who have refused repentance, and have hardened themselves against the Most High, are forever banished from their God and from all hope of peace or restoration. If your ear could be applied to the gratings of their cells, if you could walk the gloomy corridors wherein damned spirits are confined, you would then with chilled blood, and hair erect, learn what the curse of the law must be—that dread malediction which comes on the disobedient from the hand of the just and righteous God.

The curse of God is to lose God's favor; consequently, to lose the blessings which come upon that favor; to lose peace of mind, to lose hope, ultimately to lose life itself; for "the soul that sinneth, it shall die"; and that loss of life, and being cast into eternal death, is the most terrible of all, consisting as it does in everlasting separation from God and everything that makes existence truly life. A destruction lasting on forever, according to the scriptural description of it, is the fruit of the curse of the law.

O heavy tidings have I to deliver this day to some of you! Hard is my task to have to testify to you thus the terrible justice of the law. But you would not understand or prize the exceeding love of Christ if you heard not the curse from which He delivers His people; therefore hear me patiently. O unhappy men, who are under God's curse today! You may dress yourselves in scarlet and fine linen, you may go to your feasts, and drain your full bowls of wine; you may lift high the sparkling cup, and whirl in the joyous dance, but if God's curse be on you, what madness possesses you! O sirs, if you could but see it, and understand it, this curse would darken all the windows of your mirth. O that you could hear for once the voice which speaks against you from Ebal, with doleful repetition: "Cursed shalt thou be in the city, and cursed shalt thou be in the field. Cursed shall be thy basket and thy store. Cursed shall be the fruit of thy body, and the fruit of thy land, the increase of thy kine, and the flocks of thy sheep. Cursed shalt thou be when thou comest in, and cursed shalt thou be when thou goest out."

How is it you can rest while such sentences pursue you? O unhappiest of men, those who pass out of this life still accursed. One might weep tears of blood to think of them. Let our thoughts fly to them for a moment, but let us not continue in sin, lest our spirits be condemned to hold perpetual companionship in their grief. Let us fly to the dear cross of Christ, where the curse was put away, that we may never come to know in the fullness of its horror what the curse may mean.

Who Are under This Curse?

A second inquiry of great importance to us is this: WHO ARE UNDER THIS CURSE? Listen with solemn awe, O sons of men. First, especially and foremost, the Jewish nation lies under the curse, for such I gather from the connection. To them the law of God was very peculiarly given beyond all others. They heard it from Sinai, and it was to them surrounded with a golden setting of ceremonial symbol, and enforced by solemn national covenant. Moreover, there was a word in the commencement of that law which showed that in a certain sense it peculiarly belonged to Israel. "I am the Lord thy God, which brought thee out of the land of Egypt, from the house of bondage."

Paul tells us that those who have sinned without law shall be punished without law; but the Jewish nation, having received the law, if they broke it, would become peculiarly liable to the curse which was threatened for such breach. Yet further, all nations that dwell upon the face of the earth are also subject to this curse, for this reason: that if the law was not given to all from Sinai, it has been written by the finger of God more or less legibly upon the conscience of all mankind. It needs no prophet to tell an Indian, a Laplander, a South Sea Islander, that he must not steal; his own judgment so instructs him. There is that within every man which ought to convince him that idolatry is folly, that adultery and unchastity are villainies, that theft, and murder, and covetousness, are all evil.

Now, inasmuch as all men in some degree have the law within, to that degree they are under the law; the curse of the law for transgression comes upon them. Moreover, "there are some here who are peculiarly under the curse." Now, there are some of you who choose to be under the law; you deliberately choose to be judged by it. How so? Why, you are trying to reach a place in heaven by your own good works; you are clinging to the idea that something you can do can save you; you have therefore elected to be under the law, and by so doing you have chosen the curse; for all that the law of works can do for you, is to leave you still accursed, because you have not fulfilled all its commands.

O sirs, repent of so foolish a choice, and declare henceforth that you are willing to be saved by grace, and not at all by the works of the law. There is a little band here who feel the weight of the law, to whom I turn with brightest hope, though they themselves are in despair. They feel in their consciences today that they deserve from God the severest punishment; this sense of His wrath weighs them to the dust. I am glad of this, for it is only the way of escape from it. You do not know what it is to be redeemed from the curse till you have first felt the slavery of it. No man will ever rejoice in the liberty which Christ gives him till he has first felt the iron of bondage entering into his soul.

I know there are some here who say, "Let God say what He will against me, or do what He will to me, I deserve it all. If He drive me forever from His presence, and I hear the Judge pronounce that awful sentence, 'Depart, accursed one'; I can only admit that such has been my heart and such my life, that I could expect no other doom." O dear heart, if you are thus brought down, you will listen gladly to me while I now come to a far brighter theme than all this. You are under the curse as you now are, but I rejoice to have to tell you that the curse has been removed through Jesus Christ our Lord. O may the Lord lead you to see the plan of substitution and to rejoice in it.

How Was Christ Made a Curse for Us?

Our third and main point is to answer the question: HOW WAS CHRIST MADE A CURSE FOR US? The whole pith and marrow of the religion of Christianity lies in the doctrine of "substitution," and I do not hesitate to affirm my conviction that a very large proportion of Christians are not Christians at all, for they do not understand the fundamental doctrine of the Christian creed; and alas! there are preachers who do not preach, or even believe this cardinal truth. They speak of the blood of Jesus in an indistinct kind of way, and descant upon the death of Christ in a hazy style of poetry, but they do not strike this nail on the head, and lay it down that the way of salvation is by Christ's becoming a substitute for guilty man.

This shall make me the more plain and definite. Sin is an accursed thing. God, from the necessity of His holiness, must curse it; He must punish men for committing it; but the Lord's Christ, the glorious Son of the everlasting Father, became a man, and suffered in His own proper person the curse which was due to the sons of men, that so, by a vicarious offering, God having been just in punishing sin, could extend His bounteous mercy toward those who believe in the Substitute.

Now for this point. But, you inquire, how was Jesus Christ a curse? We beg you to observe the word "made." "He was *made* a curse." Christ was no curse in Himself. In His person He was spotlessly innocent, and nothing of sin could belong personally to Him. In Him was no sin. "God made him to be sin for us," the apostle expressly adds, "who knew no sin." There must never be supposed to be any degree of blameworthiness or censure in the person or character of Christ as He stands as an individual. He is in that respect without spot or wrinkle, or any such thing, the immaculate Lamb of God's Passover.

Nor was Christ made a curse of necessity. There was no necessity in Himself that He should ever suffer the curse; no necessity except that which His own loving suretyship created. His own intrinsic holiness kept Him from sin, and that same holiness kept Him from the curse. He was made sin *for us*, not on His own account, not with any view to Himself, but wholly because He loved us, and chose to put Himself in the place which we ought to have occupied.

He was made a curse for us not, again I say, out of any personal desert, or out of any personal necessity, but because He had voluntarily undertaken to be the covenant head of His people, and to be their representative, and as their representative to bear the curse which was due to them. We would be very clear here, because very strong expressions have been used by those who hold the great truth which I am endeavoring to preach, which strong expressions have conveyed the truth they meant to convey, but also a great deal more. Martin Luther's wonderful book on the Galatians, which he prized so much that he called it his Catherine Bora (that was the name of his beloved wife, and he gave this book the name of the dearest one he knew). In that book he says plainly, but be assured he did not mean what he said to be literally understood, that Jesus Christ was the greatest sinner that ever lived; that all the sins of men were so laid upon Christ that He became all the thieves, and murderers, and adulterers that ever were, in one. Now, he meant this, that God treated Christ as if He had been a great sinner; as if He had been all the sinners in the world in one; and such language teaches that truth very plainly: but, Luther, like in his boisterousness, he overshoots his mark, and leaves room for the censure that he has almost spoken blasphemy against the blessed person of our Lord.

Now, Christ never was and never could be a sinner; and in His person and in His character, in Himself considered, He never could be anything but well-beloved of God, and blessed forever and well-pleasing in Jehovah's sight; so that when we say today that He was a curse, we must lay stress on those words, "He was *made* a curse—constituted a curse, set as a curse"; and then again we must emphasize those other words, "*for us*"—not on His own account at all; but entirely out of love to us, that we might be redeemed, He stood in the sinner's place and was reckoned to be a sinner, and treated as a sinner, and made a curse for us.

Let us go farther into this truth. How was Christ made a curse? In the first place, He was made a curse because all the sins of His people were actually laid on Him. Remember the words of the apostle—it is no doctrine of mine, mark you; it is an inspired sentence, it is God's doctrine—"He made him to be sin for us"; and let me quote another passage from the prophet Isaiah, "The Lord hath laid on him the iniquity of us all"; and yet another from the same prophet, "He shall bear their iniquities." The sins of God's people were lifted from them and imputed to Christ, and their sins were looked upon us as if Christ had committed them. He was regarded as if *He* had been the sinner; He actually and in very deed stood in the sinner's place.

Next to the imputation of sin came the curse of sin. The law, looking for sin to punish, with its quick eye detected sin laid upon Christ, and, as it must curse sin wherever it was found, it cursed the sin as it was laid on Christ.

So Christ was made a curse. Wonderful and awful words, but as they are scriptural words, we must receive them. Sin being on Christ, the curse came on Christ, and in consequence, our Lord felt an unutterable horror of soul. Surely it was that horror which made Him sweat great drops of blood when He saw and felt that God was beginning to treat Him as if He had been a sinner. The holy soul of Christ shrank with deepest agony from the slightest contact with sin. So pure and perfect was our Lord that never an evil thought had crossed His mind, nor had His soul; the heart refused its healthful action, and a bloody sweat bedewed His face. Then He began to be made a curse for us, nor did He cease till He had suffered all the penalty which was due on our account.

We have been accustomed in divinity to divide that penalty into two parts, the penalty of *loss* and the penalty of actual *suffering*. Christ endured both of these. It was due to sinners that they should lose God's favor and presence, and therefore Jesus cried, "My God, my God, why hast thou forsaken me?" It was due to sinners that they should lose all personal comfort; Christ was deprived of every consolation, and even the last rag of clothing was torn from Him, and He was left like Adam naked and forlorn. It was necessary that the soul should lose everything that could sustain it, and so did Christ lose every comfortable thing; He looked and there was no man to pity or help; He was made to cry, "But I am a worm, and no man; a reproach of men, and despised of the people."

As for the second part of the punishment, namely, an actual infliction of suffering, our Lord endured this also to the uttermost, as the evangelists clearly show. You have read full often the story of His bodily sufferings; take care that you never depreciate them. There was an amount of physical pain endured by our Savior which His body never could have borne unless it had been sustained and strengthened by union with His Godhead; yet the sufferings of His soul were the soul of His sufferings.

That soul of His endured a torment equivalent to hell itself. The punishment that was due to the wicked was that of hell, and though Christ suffered not hell, He suffered an equivalent for it; and now, can your minds conceive what that must have been? It was an anguish never to be measured, an agony never to be comprehended. It is to God, and God alone that His griefs were fully known. Well does the Greek liturgy put it, "Thine unknown sufferings," for they must forever remain beyond guess of human imagination.

See, brethren, Christ has gone thus far; He has taken the *sin*, taken the *curse*, and suffered all the *penalty*. The last penalty of sin was death; and therefore the Redeemer died. Behold, the mighty Conqueror yields up His life upon the tree! His side is pierced; the blood and water flows forth, and His disciples lay His body in the tomb. As He was first numbered with the transgressors, He was afterwards numbered with the dead.

See, beloved, here is Christ bearing the curse instead of His people. Here He is coming under the load of their sin, and God does not spare Him but smites Him, as He must have smitten us, lays His full vengeance on Him, launches all His thunderbolts against Him, bids the curse wreak itself upon Him, and Christ suffers all, sustains all.

What Are the Blessed Consequences of Christ's Having Thus Been Made a Curse for Us?

And now let us conclude by considering: WHAT ARE THE BLESSED CON-SEQUENCES OF CHRIST'S HAVING THUS BEEN MADE A CURSE FOR US? The consequences are that He has redeemed us from the curse of the law. As many as Christ died for, are forever free from the curse of the law; for when the law comes to curse a man who believes in Christ, he says, "What have I to do with thee, O law? Thou sayest, 'I will curse thee,' but I reply, 'Thou hast cursed Christ instead of me. Canst thou curse twice for one offense?'" Behold how the law is silenced! God's law having received all it can demand, is not so unrighteous as to demand anything more. All that God can demand of a believing sinner, Christ has already paid, and there is no voice in earth or heaven that can henceforth accuse a soul that believes in Jesus.

You were in debt, but a friend paid your debt; no writ can be served on you. It matters nothing that *you* did not pay it, it is paid, and you have the receipt. That is sufficient in any court of equity. So with all the penalty that was due to us Christ has borne it. It is true I have not borne it; I have not been to hell and suffered the full wrath of God, but Christ has suffered that wrath for me, and I am as clear as if I had myself paid the debt to God and had myself suffered His wrath.

Here is a glorious foundation to rest upon! Here is a rock upon which to lay the basis of eternal comfort! Let a man once get to this. My Lord outside the city's gate did bleed for me as my surety, and on the cross discharged my debt. Why, then, great God, Your thunders I no longer fear. How can You smite me now? You have exhausted the quiver of Your wrath; every arrow has been already shot forth against the person of my Lord, and I am in Him clear and clean, and absolved and delivered, even as if I had never sinned.

"He hath redeemed us," says the text. How often I have heard certain gentry of the modern school of theology sneer at the atonement, because they charge us with the notion of its being a sort of business transaction, or what they choose to call "the mercantile view of it." I hesitate not to say that the mercantile metaphor expresses rightly God's view of redemption, for we find it so in Scripture; the atonement is a ransom—that is to say, a price paid; and in the present case the original word is more than usually expressive; it is a payment for, a price instead of. In His sufferings Jesus did perform what may be forcibly and fitly described as the payment of a ransom, the giving to justice a *quid pro quo* for what was due on our behalf for our sins.

Christ in His person suffered what we ought to have suffered in our persons. Our sins were made His; He stood as a sinner in God's sight; though not a sinner in Himself, He was punished as a sinner, and died as a sinner upon the tree of the curse. Then having exhausted His imputed sinnership by bearing the full penalty, He made an end of sin, and He rose again from the dead to bring in that everlasting righteousness which at this moment covers the persons of all His elect, so that they can exultingly cry, "Who shall lay anything to the charge of God's elect? It is God that justifieth. Who is He that condemneth? It is Christ that died, yea, rather, that is risen again, who is even at the right hand of God, who also maketh intercession for us."

Another blessing flows from this satisfactory substitution. It is this, that now the blessing of God, which had been hitherto arrested by the curse is made most freely to flow. Read the verse that follows the text: "That the blessing of Abraham might come on the Gentiles through Jesus Christ; that we might receive the promise of the Spirit through faith." The blessing of Abraham was that in his seed all nations of the earth should be blessed. Since our Lord Jesus Christ has taken away the curse due to sin, a great rock has been lifted out of the river-bed of God's mercy, and the living stream comes rippling, rolling, swelling on in crystal tides, sweeping before it all human sin and sorrow, and making glad the thirsty who stoop down to drink thereat.

O my brethren, the blessings of God's grace are full and free; they are as full as your necessities. Great sinners, there is great mercy for you. They are as free as your poverty could desire them to be, free as the air you breathe, or as the cooling stream that flows along the water-brook. You have but to trust Christ, and you shall live. Be you who you may, or what you may, or where you may, though at hell's dark door you lie down to despair and die, yet the message comes to you, "God hath made Christ to be a propitiation for sin. He made Him to be sin for us who knew no sin, that we might be made the righteousness of God in Him." Christ has delivered us from the curse of the law, being made a curse for us.

He who believes has no curse upon him. He may have been an adulterer, a swearer, a drunkard, a murderer, but the moment he believes, God sees none of those sins in him. He sees him as an innocent man, and regards his sins as having been laid on the Redeemer, and punished in Jesus as He died on the tree. I tell you, if you believe in Christ, my hearer, though you be the most damnable of wretches who ever polluted the earth, yet you shall not have a sin remaining on you after believing. God will look at you as pure; even Omniscience shall not detect a sin in you, for your sin shall be put on the scapegoat, even Christ, and carried away into forgetfulness, so that if your transgressions be searched for, it shall not be found. If you believe—there is the question—you are clean; if you will trust the incarnate God, you are delivered. He who believes is justified from all things. "Believe on the Lord Jesus Christ, and thou shalt be saved," for "he that believeth and is baptized, shall be saved; and he that believeth not shall be damned."

I have preached to you the gospel, God knows with what a weight upon my soul, and yet with what holy joy. This is no subject for gaudy eloquence, or for high-flying attempts at oratory; this is a matter to be put to you plainly and simply. Sinners—you must either be cursed of God, or else you must accept Christ, as bearing the curse instead of you. I do beseech you, as you love your souls, if you have any sanity left, accept this blessed and divinely appointed way of salvation. This is the truth which the apostles preached, and suffered and died to maintain; it is this for which the Reformers struggled; it is this for which the martyrs burned at Smithfield; it is the grand basic doctrine of the Reformation, and the very truth of God.

Down with your crosses and rituals, down with your pretensions to good works, and your crouchings at the feet of priests to ask absolution from them! Away with your accursed and idolatrous dependence upon yourself; Christ has finished salvation-work, altogether finished it. Hold not up your rages in competition with His fair white linen. Christ has borne the curse; bring not your pitiful penances, and your tears all full of filth to mingle with the precious fountain flowing with His blood. Lay down what is your own, and come and take what is Christ's. Put away now everything that you have thought of being or doing, by way of winning acceptance with God; humble yourselves, and take Jesus Christ to be the Alpha and Omega, the first and last, the beginning and end of your salvation. If you do this, not only shall you be saved, but you *are* saved: rest, weary one, for your sins are forgiven; rise, lame man, lame through want of faith, for your transgression is covered; rise from the dead, corrupt one, rise, like Lazarus from the tomb, for Jesus calls! Believe and live.

The words in themselves, by the Holy Spirit, are soul-quickening. Have done with tears of repentance and vows of good living, until you have come to Christ; then take them up as you will. Your first lesson should be none but Jesus, none but Jesus, none but Jesus. O come to Him! See, He hangs upon the cross; His arms are open wide, and He cannot close them, for the nails hold them fast. He waits for you; His feet are fastened to the wood, as though He meant to tarry still. O come to Him! His heart has room for you. It streams with blood and water; it was pierced for you. That mingled stream is—

> Of sin the double cure,
> To cleanse *thee* from its guilt and power.

An act of faith will bring you to Jesus. Say, "Lord, I believe, help thou mine unbelief"; and if you do, He cannot cast you out, for His word is, "Him that cometh to me I will in no wise cast out." I have delivered to you the weightiest truth that ever ears heard, or that lips spoke; put it not from you. As we shall meet each other at the last tremendous day, when heaven and earth are on a blaze, and the trumpet shall ring and raise the dead, as we shall meet each other then, I challenge you to put this from you. If you do it, it is at your own peril, and your blood be on your own heads; but the rather accept the gospel I have delivered to you. It is Jehovah's gospel. Heaven itself speaks in the words you hear today. Accept Jesus Christ as your substitute. O do it now, this moment, and God shall have glory, but you shall have salvation. Amen.

3
Christuck Made Sin[*]

For he hath made him to be sin for us who knew no sin, that we might be made the righteousness of God in him (2 Corinthians 5:21).

I daresay I have preached from this text several times in your hearing. If my life be spared, I hope to preach from it twice as many more. The doctrine it teaches, like salt upon the table, must never be left out; or like bread, which is the staff of life, it is proper at every meal.

See here the foundation-truth of Christianity, the rock on which our hopes are built. It is the only hope of a sinner, and the only true joy of the Christian—the great transaction, the great substitution, the great lifting of sin from the sinner to the sinner's Surety; the punishment of the Surety instead of the sinner; the pouring out of the vials of wrath, which were due to the transgressor, upon the head of his Substitute; the grandest transaction which ever took place on earth; the most wonderful sight that even hell ever beheld, and the most stupendous marvel that heaven itself ever executed—Jesus Christ made sin for us, that we might be made the righteousness of God in Him!

You scarcely need that I should explain the words when the sense is so plain. A spotless Savior stands in the place of guilty sinners. God lays upon the spotless Savior the sin of the guilty, so that He becomes, in the expressive language of the text, *sin*. Then He takes off from the innocent Savior His righteousness, and puts that to the account of the once-guilty sinners, so that the sinners become *righteousness*—righteousness of the highest and divinest source—*the righteousness of God in Christ Jesus.*

Of this transaction I would have you think now. Think of it *adoringly*; think of it *lovingly*; think of it *joyfully*.

---

[*] This sermon was published on Thursday, June 23, 1910, and was selected from *The Metropolitan Tabernacle Pulpit.*

Look at It with Devout Adoration

When you look at the great doctrine of substitution, you especially who are concerned in it, and can see your sins laid upon Christ, I want you to LOOK AT IT WITH DEVOUT ADORATION.

Lowly and reverently *adore the justice of God.* God set His heart upon saving your souls, but He would not be unjust, even to indulge His favorite attribute of mercy. He had purposed that you should be His; He had set His love upon you, unworthy as you are, before the foundation of the world. Yet, to save you, He would not tarnish His justice. He had said, "The soul that sinneth it shall die"; and He would not recall the word, because it was not too severe, but simply a just and righteous threatening. Sooner than He would tarnish His justice, He bound His only-begotten Son to the pillar, and scourged and bruised Him. Sooner than sin should go unpunished, He put that sin upon Christ, and punished it—O, how tremendously, and with what terrific strokes!

Christ can tell you, but probably, if He did tell you, you could not understand all that God thinks about sin, for God hates it, and loathes it, and must and will punish it; and upon His Son He laid a tremendous weight, incomprehensible, till the griefs of the dying Redeemer utterly surpassed all our imagination or comprehension. Adore, then, the justice of God, and think how you might have had to adore it, not at the foot of the cross, but in the depths of hell!

O my soul, if you had had your deserts, you would have been driven from the presence of God! Instead of looking into those languid eyes which wept for you, you would have had to look into His face whose eyes are as a flame of fire. Instead of hearing Him say, "I have blotted out thy sins," I might have heard Him say, "Depart, thou cursed one, into everlasting fire." Will you not pay as much reverence to the justice of God exhibited on the cross as exhibited in hell? Let your reverence be deeper. It will not be that of a slave, or even of a servant; but let it be quite as humble; bow low, bless the justice of God, marvel at its severity, adore its unlimited holiness, join with seraphs who surely at the foot of the cross may sing, as well as before the throne, "Holy, holy, holy, is the Lord of hosts."

While you admire the justice, *admire also the wisdom of God.* We ought to adore God's wisdom in everything we see in creation. The physician with His scalpel should adore the wisdom of God in the anatomical skill by which the human body is formed and fashioned. The traveler, as He passes through the wonders of nature, should adore the wisdom of God in the creation of the world, with its towering mountains and with its depths unknown. Every student of the works of God should account the universe as a temple in which the gorgeous outline does not excel the beauty and the holiness of all its fittings, for in the temple everything speaks of

Jehovah's glory. But, oh! at the foot of the cross, wisdom is concentrated; all its rays are concentrated there as with a burning-glass. We see God there reconciling contrary attributes as they appear to us. We see God there "glorious in holiness, fearful in praises, doing wonders," and yet "forgiving iniquity, and transgression, and sin."

He smites as though He were cruel; He forgives as though He were not just; He is as generous in passing by sin as if He were not the Judge of all the earth; He is as severe to punish sin as if He were not the tender Father who can press the prodigal to His bosom. Here you see love and justice embrace each other in such a wondrous way that I ask you to imitate the seraphs who, now that they see what they once desired to look into, veil their faces with their wings, adoring the only wise God.

Further, beloved, when you have thus thought of His justice and of His wisdom, bow your head again in reverence as you contemplate *the grace of God*. For what reason did God give His only-begotten Son to bleed instead of us? We were worms for insignificance, we were vipers for iniquity; if He saved us, were we worth the saving? We were such infamous traitors that, if He doomed us to the eternal fire, we might have been terrible examples of His wrath; but heaven's darling bleeds that earth's traitors may not bleed. Tell it; tell it in heaven, and publish it in all the golden streets every hour of every glorious day, that such is the grace of God "that he gave his only-begotten Son, that whosoever believeth in him should not perish, but have everlasting life."

And here, while I ask you to adore, I feel inclined to close the sermon, and to bow myself in silence before the grace of God in Christ Jesus. "Behold, what manner of love the Father hath bestowed upon us!" Behold it in the sweat of blood which stained Gethsemane! Behold it in the scourging which has made the name of Gabbatha a terror! Behold it in "the pains, and groans, and dying strife" of Calvary! Bow, did I say? *Prostrate* your spirits now! Lift up your sweetest music, but let your soul feel the deepest abasement as you see this super abounding grace of God in the person of the only-begotten of the Father, making Him to be sin for us who knew no sin!

When you have thus thought of His justice, His wisdom, and His grace, like a silver thread running through the whole, I want you once more to *adore His sovereignty*. What sovereignty is this, that angels who fell should have no Redeemer, but that man, insignificant man, being fallen, should find a Savior in heaven's only-begotten! See this sovereignty, too, that this precious blood should come to some of us, and not to others! Millions in this world have never heard of it. Tens of thousands, who have heard of it, have rejected it. Aye, and in this little section of the world's population encompassed now within these walls, how many there are who have had that precious blood preached in their hearing, and presented to them with loving invitations, only to reject it and despise it! And if you and I have felt the power of it, and can see the blood cleansing us from sin, shall we not admire that discriminating, distinguishing grace which has made us to differ?

But the part of sovereignty which astonishes me most is that God should have been pleased to make "*him* to be sin for us who knew no sin," that God should be pleased to ordain salvation by Christ as our Substitute. A great many persons rail at this plan of salvation; but if God has determined it, you and I ought to accept it with delight. "Behold," says God, "I lay in Zion a chief corner stone, elect, precious." The sovereignty of God has determined that no man should be saved except by the atoning sacrifice of Christ. If any man would be clean, Jehovah declares that he must wash in the fountain which Jesus filled from His veins. If God should put away sin, and accept the sinner, He declares that it should only be through that sinner putting his trust in the sacrifice offered once for all by the Lord Jesus Christ upon the tree.

Admire this sovereignty, and adore it by yielding to it. Cavil not at it. Down, rebellious will! Hush, naugthy reason, that would fain ask, "Why?" and "Wherefore? Is there no other method?" Yield, my heart! "Kiss the Son, lest he be angry, and ye perish from the way, when his wrath is kindled but a little." O magnificent love! A way as splendid as the end! A plan as glorious as its design! The design to save is not more resplendent than the method by which men are saved. Justice is magnified, wisdom extolled, grace resplendent, and every attribute of God glorified. O let us, at the very mention of a dying Savior, bow down and adore!

Look Lovingly

Not to change the topic, but to vary the line of thought, let us endeavor to LOOK LOVINGLY at Jesus Christ made sin for His people.

Every word here may help our love. That word "*Him*" may *remind us of His person*: "He hath made *him* to be sin for us,"—*Him*!—the Son of God, co-equal and co-eternal with His Father, *Him*!—the Son of Mary, born at Bethlehem, the spotless "Son of man." "He hath made *him* to be sin." I am not going to enlarge, I only want to bring His blessed person clearly before your mind. He who trod the billows, He who healed the sick, He who had compassion upon the multitudes, and fed them, He who ever lives to make intercession for us—"he hath made *him* to be sin." I am not going to enlarge, I only want to bring His blessed person before your mind. He who trod the billows, He who healed the sick, He who had compassion upon the multitudes, and fed them, He who ever lives to make intercession for us—"he hath made *him* to be sin for us." O, love Him, sinner, and let your heart join in the words, "His person fixes all my love."

I do delight to have you get a hold of Him as being verily a Person. Do not think of Him as a fiction now; aye, and never do so. Do not regard Him as a mere historical personage, who walked the stage of history, and now is gone. He is very near to you now. He is living still. We oftentimes sing—

> Crown him Lord of all.

Well, this is that self-same glorious One, "He hath made *him* to be sin for us." Think of Him, and let your love flow out toward Him.

Would you further excite your love? *Think of His character*. He knew no sin; there was none within Him, for He had none of our sinful desires and evil propensities. "Tempted in all points like as we are, yet without sin"; think of that, and then read, "He hath made *him to be sin for us*." Do not fritter that away by putting in the word "offering," and saying "sin-offering." The word stands in apposition—what if I say opposition?—to the word "righteousness" in the other part of the text. He made Him to be as much sin as He makes us to be righteousness; that is to say, He makes Him to be sin by imputation, as He makes us to be righteousness by imputation.

On Him, who never was a sinner, who never could be a sinner, our sin was laid. Consider how His holy soul must have shrunk back from being made sin, and yet, I pray you, do not fritter away the words of the prophet Isaiah, "The Lord hath laid on him the iniquity of us all." He bore our transgressions, and carried our sins in His own body on the tree. There was before the bar of justice an absolute transfer made of guilt from His elect to Himself. There He was made sin for us, though He knew no sin personally, "that we might be made the righteousness of God in Him." As you think of His pure, immaculate nature, and perfect life, love Him as you see Him bearing the burden of sins not His own, for which He came to atone.

Will not your love be excited when you *think of the difficulty of this imputation*? "He hath *made him* to be sin." None but God could have put sin upon Christ. It is well said that there is no lifting of sin from one person to another. There is no such thing as far as we are concerned; but things which are impossible with man are possible with God. Do you know what it means for Christ to be made sin? You do not, but you can form some guess of what it involves; for, when He was made sin, God treated Him as if He had been a sinner, which He never was, and never could be. God left Him as He would have left a sinner, till He cried out, "My God, my God, why hast thou forsaken me?" God smote Him as He would have smitten a sinner, till His soul was "exceeding sorrowful, even unto death."

That which was due from His people for sin, or an equivalent to that, was literally exacted at the hands of Jesus Christ, the Son of God. He was made a debtor for our debts, and He paid them. You may guess what it was to be a debtor for us by the pain which it cost to discharge our liabilities. He that is a surety shall smart for it, and Jesus found that proverb true. When justice came to smite the sinner, it found Him in the sinner's place, and smote Him without relenting, laying to the full the whole weight upon Him which had otherwise crushed all mankind forever into the lowermost hell. Let us love Jesus as we think how He endured all this.

Beloved in the Lord, there is one more string of your harp I would like to touch, and it is *the thought of what you now are*, which the text speaks of. You are made the righteousness of God in Christ. God sees no sin in you, believer. He has put your sin, or that which was yours, to the account of Christ, and you are innocent before Him. Moreover, He sees you to be righteous. You are not perfectly righteous; the work of His Spirit in you is incomplete as yet; but He looks upon you, not as you are in yourselves, but as you are in Christ Jesus, and you are "accepted in the Beloved"; you are in His sight without spot, or wrinkle, or any such thing. What Jesus did is set to your account. He sees His Son in you, and then He loves you as He loves His Son. He has put you into union with His Son, and you are now hid with Christ in God. I trust you will endeavor to realize this position of yourselves as made the righteousness of God in Christ, and when you do, surely you will love the Savior who has done all this for you, undeserving, helpless, dying guilty mortals. O that the Lord Jesus would now send fire into all your souls, and make you love Him, for, surely, if you have but the sense of what He has done, and how He did it, and what it cost Him to do it, and who He is that has done it, and who you were for whom He has done it, you will surely say, "O for a thousand hearts that I may love thee as I would, and a thousand tongues that I may praise thee as I should!"

View the Glorious Fact of Substitution Joyfully

And now, let us VIEW THE GLORIOUS FACT OF SUBSTITUTION JOYFULLY. Here I will commence with the observation that, *till your sin as a believer is gone, and till, as a believer, Christ's righteousness is at present your glorious dress, your salvation is in no sense realized by yourselves*. It is not dependent upon your frames and feelings. Your sins are not put away through your repentance. That repentance becomes to you the token of the pardon of sin; but the true cleansing is found, not in the eyes of the penitent, but in the wounds of Jesus. Your sins were virtually discharged upon the accursed tree. You stand this day accepted, not for anything you are, or can be, or shall be, but entirely and wholly through the blood and righteousness of Jesus Christ. We cannot state this truth, it seems to me, too boldly. This is the very doctrine of the Reformation—justification by faith, or rather the basic doctrine upon which it rests; and I am persuaded the more plainly it is preached the better, for it is the gospel of salvation to a lost and ruined world.

Beloved, your case is something similar to this. You are in debt, and, according to the old laws, you must be cast into prison. You are brought up before the court; you cannot plead that you are not in debt; you are compelled to stand there, and say, "Each one of these charges I must admit; these liabilities I have incurred, and I have not a single penny with which to meet them." A friend in court, wealthy and generous, pays the debt. Now, the only reason why you go out of court clear lies in the payment made by your friend.

You do not leave the court because you never incurred the debt; nay, you did incur the debt, and you must admit that you did not leave the court because you pleaded not guilty, or because you promised never to get into debt again. Not so; all that would not have answered your purpose. Your creditor would still have cast you into prison. You did not leave the court because your character is excellent, or you hope to make it so. The only ground of your liberation from your liabilities is found in the fact that another person has discharged them for you, and that will not be affected by any act you may have committed or shall commit. You may have felt ill today; you might have labored under twenty diseases, but those diseases will not imprison you, neither will they help to set you free. Your freedom hinges upon the fact that the debt was paid for you by another.

Now, Christian, here your hope and comfort hang. This is the diamond rivet which anchors your salvation firmly. Jesus died for you; and those for whom Jesus died, in the sense in which we now use the language, are and must be saved. Unless eternal justice can punish two persons for one offense; unless eternal justice can demand payment twice for the same debt—first from the bleeding Surety, and then from those for whom the Surety stood—they must be clear for whom Jesus died. This is the gospel which we preached.

O happy they who have received it, for it is their joy to know it, sinners though they have been, guilty and ruined, and sinners though they are still; yet, since they have believed, Christ is theirs, Christ took their sins, and paid their debts; and God Himself can bring no charge against the man who is justified by Christ. "Who shall lay anything to the charge of God's elect? It is God that justifieth. Who is He that condemneth? It is Christ that died, yea, rather, that is risen again, who is even at the right hand of God, who also maketh intercession for us."

Now, Christian, I want you to come and enjoy this. Why, *it ought to make your soul dance for joy within you to think that sin is pardoned, and righteousness is imputed to you.* This is an unchanging fact, that Christ has saved you. If it was ever a fact, it is always a fact. If it was ever true, it is always true, and always alike true, as true now that you are depressed as yesterday when you were rejoicing. Jesus' blood does not change like your poor heart. It does not go up and down in value, like the markets, and fluctuate like your faith. If you are saved, you are saved. If you are resting in the blood, you are as safe today as you were yesterday, and you are as safe forever.

Remember that this is true of all the saints alike. It is true to great saints, but equally so to little ones. They all stand under this crimson canopy, and are alike protected by its blessed shadow from the beams of divine justice. It is true to you *now*. O beloved, try to live up to it! Say, "Away, my doubts; away, my fears; I trust a Savior slain, and I am saved! Away, my questionings; away, my carnal reasonings! I hate my sins, but I cannot doubt my Savior. It is true I have not lived as a Christian should live, but I will still cast myself into His arms." It is not faith to trust God as a saint when you feel you are a saint. Faith is to trust Christ as a sinner, while you are conscious that you are a sinner. To come to Jesus, and to think yourselves pure, is a sorry coming to Him; but to come with all your impurity, this is true coming.

I say to you, sinner; I say to you, saint; I say to you all this one thing, and I have done. When your souls are at the blackest, seek for nothing but the blood. When your souls are at the darkest, seek no light anywhere but in the cross. Do not cling to preparations, to humblings, to repentings. All these things are good in their way, but they cannot be a balsam to a wounded conscience. Christ and Christ crucified is what you want. Do not look within; look without. I say, when you repent, it is a base repentance that will not let you trust Christ, for while repentance should have one eye on sin, it should have the other upon the cross. While repentance should make you lie low, yet it is not repentance, but unbelief, that makes you doubt the power of Christ to save you.

Christ never came to save the righteous; He came to save sinners. I would have you magnify the grace of God by believing that, when your sin stares you most in the face, when you are most conscious of it, and it seems to be worse than ever, Christ is the same to you and for you, your glorious Surety and your blessed satisfaction. Still believe, and still trust, and do not let go your confidence that Christ is able to save sinners, even the chief, and will save you without help from your doings or feelings. His own right arm will get to Himself the victory, and, having trodden the winepress of divine wrath alone, He will save you solely by the merit of His life and of His death. O for grace to rest in the Savior, and to know the truth of this text, "He hath made him to be sin for us who knew no sin, that we might be made the righteousness of God in him."

4
*Christk Lifted Up**

And I, if I be lifted up, will draw all men unto me (John 12:32).

It was an extraordinary occasion upon which the Savior uttered these words. It was the crisis of the world. We very often speak of the "present crisis of affairs," and it is very common for persons of every period to believe their own age to be the crisis and turning point of the whole world's history. They rightly imagine that much of the future depends upon their present exertions; but they wrongly stretch the thought, and imagine that the period of their existence is the very hinge of the history of the world: that it is *the* crisis. Now, however, it may be correct, in a modified sense, that every period of time is in some sense a crisis, yet there never was a time which could be truly called a crisis, in comparison with the season when our Savior spoke. In the verse immediately preceding my text, we find in the English translation, "Now is the judgment of this world" (v. 31); but we find in the Greek, "Now is the *crisis* of this world."

The world had come to a solemn crisis: now was the great turning point of all the world's history. Should Christ die, or should He not? If He should refuse the bitter cup of agony, the world is doomed; if He should pass onward, do battle with the powers of death and hell, and come off a victor, then the world is blessed, and her future shall be glorious. Shall He succumb? Then is the world crushed and ruined beneath the trail of the serpent. Shall He conquer? Shall He lead captivity captive, and receive gifts for men? Then this world shall yet see times when there shall be "a new heaven and a new earth, wherein dwelleth righteousness."

"Now is the crisis of this world!" "The crisis," He says, "is twofold. Dealing with Satan and men. I will tell you the result of it. 'Now shall the prince of this world be cast out.' Fear not that hell shall conquer. I shall cast him out; and, on the other hand doubt not that I shall be victorious over the hearts of men. 'I, if I be lifted up, will draw all men unto me.'"

* This sermon was preached on Sunday morning, July 5, 1857, at the Music Hall, Royal Surrey Gardens. It is taken from *The New Park Street Pulpit*.

Remembering the occasion upon which these words were uttered, we shall now proceed to a discussion of them.

We have three things to notice. *Christ crucified, Christ's glory.* He calls it a lifting Him up. *Christ crucified, the minister's theme.* It is the minister's business to lift Christ up in the gospel. *Christ crucified, the heart's attraction.* "I, if I be lifted up, will draw all men unto me." *His own glory— the minister's theme—the heart's attraction.*

Christ's Crucifixion Is Christ's Glory

I begin then: CHRIST'S CRUCIFIXION IS CHRIST'S GLORY. He uses the word "lifted up" to express the manner of His death. "I, if I be lifted up, will draw all men unto me. This he said, signifying what death he should die." But notice the choice of the word to express His death. He does not say, I, if I be crucified; I, if I be hanged on the tree; no, but "I, if I be lifted up": and in the Greek there is the meaning of exaltation. "I, if I be exalted—I, if I be lifted on high." He took the outward and visible fashion of the cross, it being a lifting of Him up, to be the type and symbol of the glory with which the cross should invest even Him. "I, if I be lifted up."

Now, *the cross of Christ is Christ's glory.* We will show you how. Man seeks to win his glory by the slaughter of others—Christ by the slaughter of Himself: men seek to get crowns of gold—He sought a crown of thorns: men think that glory lies in being exalted over others—Christ thought that His glory did lie in becoming "a worm and no man," a scoff and reproach amongst all that beheld Him. He stooped when He conquered; and He counted that the glory lay as much in the stooping as in the conquest.

Christ was glorified on the cross, we say, first, *because love is always glorious.* If I might prefer any glory, I should ask to be beloved by men. Surely, the greatest glory that a man can have among his fellows is not that of mere admiration, when they stare at him as he passes through the street, and throng the avenues to behold him as he rides in his triumph; the greatest fame, the greatest glory of a patriot is the love of his country—to feel that young men and maidens, old men and sires, are prepared to fall at his feet in love, to give up all they have to serve him who has served them. Now, Christ won more love by the cross than He did ever win elsewhere. O Lord Jesus, You would never have been so much loved, if You had sat in heaven forever, as You are now loved since You have stooped to death. Not cherubim and seraphim, and angels clad in light, ever could have loved with hearts so warm as Your redeemed above, or even Your redeemed below. You won love more abundantly by the nail than by the scepter. Your own side brought You no emptiness of love, for Your people love You with all their hearts. Christ won glory by His cross. He was never so lifted up as when He was cast down; and the Christian will bear witness, that though He loves His Master anywhere, yet nothing moves His heart to rapture and vehemence of love like the story of the crucifixion and the agonies of Calvary.

Again: Christ at this time won much glory *by fortitude.* The cross was a trial of Christ's fortitude and strength, and therein it was a garden in which His glory might be planted. The laurels of His crown were sown in a soil that was saturated with His own blood. Sometimes the ambitious soldier pants for battle, because in days of peace he cannot distinguish himself. "Here I sit," says he, "and rust my sword in my scabbard, and win no glory; let me rush to the cannon's mouth; though some call honor a painted bauble, it may be so, yet I am a solider, and I want it"; and he longs for the encounter that he may win glory.

Now, in an infinitely higher sense than the poor glory which the soldier gets, Christ looked upon the cross as being His way to honor. "Oh!" said He, "now shall be the time of my endurance: I have suffered much, but I shall suffer more, and then shall the world see what a strong heart of love I have." How patient is the Lamb, how mighty to endure. Never would Christ have had such pæans of praise and such songs of honor as He now wins, if He had avoided the conflict, and the battle, and the agony. We might have blessed Him for what He is and for what He wished to do; we might have loved Him for the very longings of His heart; but we never could have praised Him for His strong endurance, for His intrepid spirit, for His unconquerable love, if we had not seen Him put to the severe test of crucifixion and the agonies of that awful day. Christ did win glory by His being crucified.

Again: Christ looked upon His crucifixion *as the completion of all His work*, and therefore He looked upon it as an exaltation. The completion of an enterprise is the harvest of its honor. Though thousands have perished in the Arctic regions, and have obtained fame for their intrepid conduct, yet, my friends, the man who at last discovers the passage is the most of all honored; and though we shall forever remember those bold men who pushed their way through winter in all its might, and dared the perils of the deep, yet the man who accomplishes the deed wins more than his share of the glory. Surely the accomplishment of an enterprise is just the point where the honor hangs.

And, my hearers, Christ longed for the cross, because He looked for it as the goal of all His exertions. It was to be the place upon which He could say, "It is finished." He could never say "It is finished" on His throne: but on His cross He did cry it. He preferred the sufferings of Calvary to the honors of the multitude who crowded around Him; for, preach as He might, and bless them as He might, and heal them as He might, still was His work undone. He was straitened; He had a baptism to be baptized with, and how was He straitened till it was accomplished. "But," He said, "now I long for my cross, for it is the topstone of my labor. I long for my sufferings,

because they shall be the completion of my great work of grace."
Brethren, it is the end that brings the honor; it is the victory that crowns the
warrior rather than the battle. And so Christ longed for this, His death, that
He might see the completion of His labor. "Aye," said He, "when I am crucified, I am exalted, and lifted up."

And, once again, Christ looked upon His crucifixion with the eye of
firm faith *as the hour of triumph.* His disciples thought that the cross would
be a degradation; Christ looked through the outward and visible, and
beheld the spiritual. "The cross," said He, "the gibbet of My doom may
seem to be cursed with ignominy, and the world shall stand round and hiss
at the crucified; My name be forever dishonored as one who died upon the
tree; and cavilers and scoffers may forever throw this in the teeth of My
friends that I died with the malefactor; but I do not look at the cross as you
do. I know its ignominy, but I despise the shame—I am prepared to endure
it all. I look upon the cross as the gate of triumph, as the portal of victory.
O shall I tell you what I shall behold upon the cross?—just when Mine eye
is swimming with the last tear, and when My heart is palpitating with its
last pang; just when My body is rent with its last thrill of anguish, then
Mine eye shall see the head of the dragon broken, it shall see hell's tow-
ers dismantled and its castle fallen. Mine eye shall see My seed eternally
saved, I shall behold the ransomed coming from their prison-houses. In that
last moment of My doom, when My mouth is just preparing for its last cry
of 'It is finished'; I shall behold the year of My redeemed come, I shall
shout triumph in the delivery of all My beloved! Aye, and I shall see then,
the world, Mine own earth conquered, and usurpers all disthroned, and I
shall behold in vision the glories of the latter days, when I shall sit upon the
throne of My father David and judge the earth, attended with the pomp of
angels and the shouts of My beloved!"

Yes, Christ saw in His cross the victories of it, and therefore did He
long for it as being the place of victory and the means of conquest. "I," said
Jesus, "if I be lifted up, if I be exalted"; He puts His crucifixion as being
His glory. This is the first point of our text.

The Minister's Main Theme

But, now, secondly, Christ has another lifting up, not ignominious, but
truly honorable; there is a lifting of Him upon the pole of the gospel, in the
preaching of the Word. Christ Jesus is to be lifted up every day; for that
purpose He came into the world: "That like as Moses lifted up the serpent
in the wilderness," even so He might by the preaching of the truth be lifted up, "that whosoever believeth in him should not perish, but have
everlasting life." Christ is THE MINISTER'S GREAT THEME, in opposition to
a thousand other things which most men choose. I would prefer that the
most prominent feature in my ministry should be the preaching of Christ

Jesus. Christ should be most prominent, *not hell and damnation.* God's ministers must preach God's terrors as well as God's mercies; we are to preach the thunder of God's law. If men will sin, we are to tell them that they must be punished for it. If they will transgress, woe unto the watchman who is ashamed to say, "The Lord cometh that taketh vengeance."

We should be unfaithful to the solemn charge which God has given us if we were wickedly to stifle all the threatenings of God's Word. Does God say, "The wicked shall be cast into hell, with all the nations that forget God"? It is our business to say so. Did the loving Savior talk of the pit that burns, of the worm that never dies, and of the fire that can never be extinguished? It is ours to speak as He spoke, and not to mince the matter. It is no mercy to men to hide their doom.

But, my brethren, terrors never ought to be the prominent feature of a minister's preaching. Many old divines thought they would do a great deal of good by preaching this. I do not believe it. Some souls are awakened and terrified by such preaching; they, however, are but few. Sometimes, right solemnly, the sacred mysteries of eternal wrath must be preached, but far oftener let us preach the wondrous love of God. There are more souls won by wooing than by threatening. It is not hell, but Christ, we desire to preach. O sinners, we are not afraid to tell you of your doom, but we do not choose to be forever dwelling on that doleful theme. We rather love to tell you of Christ, and Him crucified. We want to have our preaching rather full of the frankincense of the merits of Christ than of the smoke, and fire, and terrors of Mount Sinai. We are not come unto Mount Sinai, but unto Mount Zion—where milder words declare the will of God, and rivers of salvation are abundantly flowing.

Again, the theme of a minister should be Christ Jesus *in opposition to mere doctrine.* Some of my good brethren are always preaching doctrine. Well, they are right in so doing, but I would not care myself to have as the characteristic of my preaching, doctrine only. I would rather have it said, "He dwelt much upon the person of Christ, and seemed best pleased when he began to tell about the atonement and the sacrifice. He was not ashamed of the doctrine, he was not afraid of threatening, but he seemed as if he preached the threatening with tears in his eyes, and the doctrine solemnly as God's own word; but, when he preached of Jesus, his tongue was loosed, and his heart was at liberty." Brethren, there are some who preach the doctrine only, who are an injury, I believe, to God's church rather than a benefit. I know of some who have set themselves up as umpires over all spirits. They are *the* last word. Wisdom will die with them. If they were once taken away, the great standard of truth would be removed. We do not wonder that they hate the Pope, two of a trade never agree, for they are far more popish than he, they being themselves infallible. I am afraid that very much of the soundness of this age, is but a mere sound, and is not real;

does not enter into the core of the heart, nor affect the being. Brethren, we would rather preach Christ than election. We love election, we love predestination, we love the great doctrines of God's Word, but we had rather preach Christ than preach these. We desire to put Christ above doctrine, we make the doctrine the throne for Christ to sit on, but we dare not put Christ at the bottom, and then press Him down, and overload Him with the doctrines of His own Word.

And again, the minister ought to preach Christ *in opposition to mere morality*. How many ministers in London could preach as well out of Shakespeare as the Bible, for all they want is a moral maxim. They never think of mentioning regeneration. Sometimes the preacher talks of moral renovation. He does not think of talking about perseverance by grace. No; continuance in well-doing is his perpetual cry. He does not think of preaching "believe and be saved." No; his continual exhortation is, "Good Christian people, say your prayers, and behave well, and by these means you shall enter the kingdom of heaven."

The sum and substance of his gospel is that we can do very well without Christ, that although certainly there is a little amiss in us, yet if we just mend our ways in some little degree, that old text, "except a man be born again," need not trouble us. If you want to be made drunkards, if you want to be made dishonest, if you want to be taught every vice in the world, go and hear a moral preacher. These gentlemen, in their attempts to reform and make people moral, are the men that lead them from morality. Hear the testimony of holy Bishop Lavington, "We have long been attempting to reform the nation by moral preaching. With what effect? None. On the contrary, we have dexterously preached the people into downright infidelity. We must change our voice; we must preach Christ and Him crucified; nothing but the gospel is the power of God unto salvation."

And yet one more remark. The minister ought to preach Christ in opposition to some who think they ought to preach *learning*. God forbid we should ever preach against learning. The more of it a man can get, the better for him, and the better for his hearers if he has grace enough to use it well. But there are some who have so much of learning, that if in the course of their readings they find a very hard word, out comes the pencil-case: they jot it down, to be glorified in the next Sunday morning's sermon. Do they find out some outlandish German expression, which, if pulled to pieces, would mean nothing, but which looks as if it must be something wonderful, that must always come out, if all the gospel go to the wall. You ought to pray to God that they may never be allowed to read anything but their Bibles all the week because then you might hear something you could understand. But this would not suit his reverence; if he could be understood, he would not be a great preacher, for a great preacher, according to the opinion of some, is a man who is called intellectual—that is to say, a man who knows more about the Bible than the Bible knows about itself; a man who can explain all mysteries by intellect merely, who smiles at anything like unction and savor, or the influence of God's Spirit as being mere fanaticism. Intellect with him is everything. You sit and hear him, you go out, "Dear me, what a remarkable man he is. I suppose he made something out of the text, but I did not know what it was. He seemed to me to be in a fog himself, although I admit it was an extremely luminous haze." Then people will go again and be sure to take a pew in that church, because they say he is such a clever man. The only reason is that they cannot understand him.

In reading the other day a book of advice to ministers, I found it stated, and very gravely too, by some good old tutor of a college, "Always have one part of your sermon which the vulgar cannot comprehend, because in that way you will have a name for learning, and what you say that they *can* understand, will impress them the more, for by putting in a sentence or two which is incomprehensible, you at once strike their minds as being a superior man, and they believe in the weight and the authority of your learning, and, therefore, give credence to the rest which they can comprehend." Now, I hold that is all wrong. Christ wants us not to preach *learning*, but to preach the good word of life in the simplest manner possible. Why, if I could only get lords and ladies to listen to me, by preaching to them so that they alone could understand me, there! they might go, and I would not so much as snap my finger for them all. I would desire so to preach that the servant maid can understand, that the coachman can understand, that the poor and illiterate may hear readily and gladly receive the word.

And mark you, there never will be much good come to the ministry until it is simplified, until our brethren learn one language, which they do not seem to know. Latin, Greek, French, Hebrew, and twenty other languages they know. There is one I would recommend to their very serious study—it is called English. If they would just try and learn that, it is astonishing what a mighty language they would find it to move the hearts of men. English before every language in the world. When every other has died out for want of power, Saxon will live, and triumph with its iron tongue, and its voice of steel. We must have the common, plain language in which to address the people. And mark this, we must have Christ lifted up, Christ crucified, without the gauds and fripperies of learning, without the trappings of attempted eloquence or oratory. If Christ Jesus be earnestly preached, He will draw all men unto Him.

And now we go to the third point, which is, indeed, the essence of the text.

The Attractive Power of the Cross of Christ

If Christ be thus preached, thus fully held forth, thus simply proclaimed to the people, the effect will be, He will draw all men unto Him. Now, I

will show THE ATTRACTING POWER OF CHRIST in three or four ways. Christ
draws *like a trumpet* attracting men to hear the proclamation. Christ draws
like a net bringing men out of the sea of sin. Christ draws, also, *with bonds
of love*. In the next place, Christ attracts *like a standard*, bringing all the
soldiers round Him, and, in the last place, Christ draws *like a chariot*. "I,
if I be lifted up, I will draw all men unto me." Now, I will try if I can show
these points.

First, I said that Christ draws *as a trumpet*. Men have been wont to
sound a trumpet to attract an audience to the reading of a proclamation. The
people come from their houses at the well-known sound, to listen to what
they are desired to know. Now, my brethren, part of the attractive power
of the gospel lies in attracting people to hear it. You cannot expect people
to be blessed by the preaching of the gospel if they do not hear it. One part
of the battle is to get them to listen to its sound. Now, the question is asked
in these times, "How are we to get the working-classes to listen to the
Word?" The answer is, Christ is His own attraction, Christ is the only trumpet that you want to trumpet Christ. Preach the gospel, and the
congregation will come of themselves. The only infallible way of getting
a good congregation is to do this. "Oh!" said a Socinian once, to a good
Christian minister, "I cannot make it out; my chapel is always empty, and
yours always crammed full. And yet I am sure mine is the more rational
doctrine, and you are not by any means so talented a preacher as I am"—
"Well," said the other, "I will tell you the reason why your chapel is empty,
and mine full. The people have a conscience, and that conscience tells them
that what I preach is true, and that what you preach is false, so they will not
hear you." You shall look through the history of this realm ever since the
commencement of the days of Protestantism, and I will dare to say it without fear of contradiction, that you will almost in every case find that the
men who have attracted the greatest mass of people to hear them, have
been men who were the most evangelical—who preached the most about
Christ and Him crucified.

What was there in Whitefield to attract an audience, except the simple
gospel preached with a vehement oratory that carried everything before it?
O, it was not his oratory, but the gospel that drew the people. There is
something about the truth that always makes it popular. For tell me that if
a man preaches the truth his chapel will be empty. Sir, I defy you to prove
that. Christ preached His own truth, and the common people heard Him
gladly, and the multitude flocked to listen to Him. My good ministering
brother, you have an empty church? Do you want to fill it? I will give you
a good recipe, and if you will follow it, you will, in all probability, have
your chapel full to the doors. Burn all your manuscripts, that is No. 1. Give
up your notes, that is No. 2. Read your Bible and preach it as you find it in
the simplicity of its language. And give up all your Latinized English.

Begin to tell the people what you have felt in your own heart, and beseech the Holy Spirit to make your heart as hot as a furnace for zeal. Then go amongst men. Tell them what you have felt and what you know, and tell it heartily with a good, bold face; and, my dear friend, I do not care who you are, you will get a congregation.

But if you say, "Now, to get a congregation, I must buy an organ." That will not serve you a bit. "But we must have a good choir." I would not care to have a congregation that comes through a good choir. "No," says another, "but really I must a little alter my style of preaching." My dear friend, it is not the style of preaching, it is the style of *feeling*. People sometimes begin to mimic other preachers, because they are successful. Why, the worst preachers are those who mimic others, whom they look upon as standards. Preach naturally. Preach out of your hearts just what you feel to be true, and the old soul-stirring words of the gospel will soon draw a congregation. "Where the body is, thither will the eagles be gathered together."

But if it ended there, what would be the good of it? If the congregation came and listened to the sound, and then went away unsaved, of what use would it be? But in the next place, Christ acts *as a net* to draw men unto Him. The gospel ministry is, in God's Word, compared to a fishery; God's ministers are the fishermen, they go to catch souls, as fishermen go to catch fish. How shall souls be caught? They shall be caught by preaching Christ. Just preach a sermon that is full of Christ, and throw it unto your congregation, as you throw a net into the sea—you need not look where they are, nor try to fit your sermon to different cases; but, throw it in, and as sure as God's Word is what it is, it shall not return to Him void; it shall accomplish that which He pleases, and prosper in the thing whereto He sent it. The gospel never was unsuccessful yet, when it was preached with the demonstration of the Spirit and of power. It is not fine orations upon the death of princes, or the movements of politics which will save souls. If we wish to have sinners saved and to have our churches increased; if we desire the spread of God's kingdom, the only thing whereby we can hope to accomplish the end, is the lifting up of Christ; for, "I, if I be lifted up, will draw all men unto me."

In the next place, Christ Jesus draws *as the cords of love*. After men are saved, they are still apt to go astray; it needs a cord to reach all the way from a sinner to heaven; and it needs to have a hand pulling at him all the way. Now, Christ Jesus is the band of love that draws the saint to heaven. O child of God, you would go astray again if Jesus did not hold you fast; if He did not draw you to Himself you would still wander. Christian people are like our earth. Our world has two forces; it has one tendency to run off at a tangent from its orbit; but the sun draws it by a centripetal power and attracts it to itself, and so between the two forces it is kept in a perpetual circle. O Christian, you will never walk aright, and keep in the orbit of truth, if it be not for the influence of Christ perpetually attracting you to the center. You feel, and if you do not feel always, it is still there—you *feel* an attraction between your heart and Christ, and Christ is perpetually drawing you to Himself, to His likeness, to His character, to His love, to His bosom, and in that way you are kept from your natural tendency to fly off and to be lost in the wide fields of sin. Bless God, that Christ lifted up draws all His people unto Him in that fashion.

And now, in the next place Christ Jesus is the center of attraction; even *as a standard* is the center of gathering. We want unity in these days; we are now crying out, "away with sectarianism." O for unity! there are some of us who truly long after it. We do not talk about an evangelical alliance; alliances are made between men of different countries. We believe that the phrase "Evangelical Alliance" is a faulty one; it should be "Evangelical Union," knit together in Union. Why! I am not in alliance with a brother of the Church of England; I would not be in alliance with him if he were ever so good a man! I would be in union with him, I would love him with all my heart, but I would not make a mere *alliance* with him. He never was my enemy, he never shall be; and, therefore, it is not an alliance I want with him—it is a *union*.

And so with all God's people, they do not care about alliances; they love real union and communion one with another. Now, what is the right way to bring all the churches to union? "We must revise the prayer book," says one. You may revise it, and revise it as long as ever you like, you will never bring some of us to agree to it, for we hate Prayer Books as such, however near perfection. "Well then, we must revise the doctrines, so that they may meet all classes." You cannot; that is impossible. "Well then, we must revise the discipline." Yes, sweep the Augean stable. And then after that, the mass of us will stand as much aloof as ever. "No, but we must each of us make mutual concession." Indeed, I wonder who will, except the Vicars of Bray, who have no principle at all. For if we have to make mutual concession, who can be guarantee that I must not concede a part of what I believe to be true? And that I cannot do, nor can my brother on the opposite side.

The only standard of union that can ever be lifted up in England is the cross of Christ. As soon as we shall begin to preach Christ and Him crucified, we shall be all one. We can fight anywhere except at the foot of the cross—there it is that the order goes forth, "sheath swords"; and those who were bitter combatants before, come and prostrate themselves there, and say, "O dear Redeemer, you have melted us into one." O my brethren, let us all preach the gospel mightily, and there will be union! The church of England is becoming more united with dissenters. Our good friends at Exeter Hall have gone a very long way to bless the world, and uproot the exclusiveness of their own system. As sure as ever they are alive they have taken the most excellent step in the world to pull down the absurd pretensions of some of their own brethren, to the exclusive claim of being "the Church." I glory and rejoice in it! I bless God for that movement, and I pray that the day may come when every bishop may do the same. And I do not glory in it merely, because I look upon it as the beginning of union, but because of the preaching of the gospel.

But, at the same time, I know this, let their example be followed, and the barriers between dissenters and the church of England are not tenable. Even the nationality of Episcopacy must yet come down. If my lord, the bishop of so and so, is to have so many thousands a year for preaching to a number of people in Exeter Hall, I have as much right as he has to a State grant; for I serve as many Englishmen as he does. There is no one church in the world that has any right to take a farthing of national money any more than I have. And if there are ten thousand gathered here, it is an unrighteous thing that we should have no subsidy from the State, when a paltry congregation of thirteen and a half in the City of London is to be supported out of national money. The thing cannot be held long, it is impossible; Christ's church will one day reject the patronage of the States.

Let all of us begin to preach the gospel, and we shall soon see that the gospel is self-supporting; and that the gospel does not want entrenchments of bigotry and narrow-mindedness, in order to make it stand. No, we shall say, "Brother, there is my pulpit for you. You are an Episcopalian, preach in my pulpit, you are right welcome to it."

The Episcopalian will say, "You are a Baptist, and my brother, there is the parish church for you." And I just announce that the first chance I get to preach in a parish church, I will do it, and risk the consequence. They are our structures, they belong to all England, we can give them to whom we please, and if tomorrow the will of the sovereign people should transfer those edifices to another denomination, there is nothing in the world that can prevent it. But if not, by what law of Christian love is one denomination to shut its pulpit doors against every other? Many of my dear friends in the Episcopal Church are willing to lend their edifices, but they dare not. But mark you, when the gospel is preached fully, all those things will be broken down. For one brother will say, "My dear friend, you preach Christ and so do I, I cannot shut you out of my pulpit." And another will cry, "I am anxious for the salvation of souls, and so are you, come into my house, come into my heart, I love you."

The only means of unity we shall ever get will be all of us preaching Christ crucified; when that is done, when every minister's heart is in the right place, full of anxiety for souls—when every minister feels that, be he called bishop, presbyter, or preacher—all he wants to do is to glorify God and win souls to Jesus, then, my dear friends, we can maintain our denominational distinctions, but the great bugbear of bigotry and division will have ceased and schism will no more be known. For that day I anxiously pray; may God send it in His own time. As far as I am concerned there is my hand for every minister of God in creation, and my heart with it, I love all who love the Lord Jesus Christ. And I feel persuaded that the nearer we all of us come to the one point of putting Christ first, Christ last, and Christ midst, and Christ without end—the nearer we shall come to the unity of the one Church of Christ in the bond of holy permanence.

And now I close by noticing the last sweet thought—"I, if I be lifted up, will draw all men unto me." Then Christ Jesus will draw all His people to heaven; He says He will draw them unto Himself. He is in heaven; then *Christ is the chariot* in which souls are drawn to heaven. The people of the Lord are on their way to heaven, they are carried in everlasting arms; and those arms are the arms of Christ. Christ is carrying them up to His own house, to His own throne; by-and-by His prayer—"Father, I will that they, whom thou hast given me be with me where I am," shall be wholly fulfilled. And it is fulfilling now, for He is like a strong courser drawing His children in the chariot of the covenant of grace unto Himself. O blessed be God, the cross is the plank on which we swim to heaven; the cross is the great covenant transport which will weather out the storms, and reach its desired heaven. This is the chariot, the pillars wherewith are of gold, and the bottom thereof silver; it is lined with the purple of the atonement of our Lord Jesus Christ.

And now, poor sinner, I would to God Christ would pardon you; remember His death on Calvary, remember His agonies and bloody sweat—all this He did for you; if you feel yourself to be a sinner. Does not this draw you to Him?

> Though thou art guilty, He is good,
> He'll wash thy soul in Jesus' blood.

You have rebelled against Him, and revolted, but He says, "return, backsliding children." Will not His love draw you? I pray that both may have their power and influence, that you may be drawn to Christ now, and at last be drawn to heaven. May God give a blessing for Jesus' sake. Amen.

5
*Christn Crucified**

*But we preach Christ crucified, unto the Jews a stumblingblock, and
unto the Greeks foolishness; but unto them which are called, both
Jews and Greeks, Christ the power of God, and the wisdom of God
(1 Corinthians 1:23,24).*

What contempt God poured upon the wisdom of this world! How He
brought it to nought, and made it appear as nothing. He has
allowed it to work out its own conclusions, and prove its own
folly. Men boasted that they were wise; they said that they could find out God
to perfection; and in order that their folly might be refuted once and forever,
God gave them the opportunity of so doing. He said, "Worldly wisdom, I will
try you. You say you are mighty, that your intellect is vast and comprehensive, that your eye is keen, that you can unravel all secrets; now, behold, I try
you: I give you one great problem to solve. Here is the universe; stars make
its canopy, fields and flowers adorn it, and the floods roll over its surface; My
name is written therein; the invisible things of God may be clearly seen in the
things which are made. Philosophy, I give you this problem—find Me out.
Here are My works—find Me out. Discover in the wondrous world which I
have made, the way to worship Me acceptably. I give you space enough to do
it—there are data enough. Behold the clouds, the earth, and the stars. I give
you time enough; I will give you four thousand years, and I will not interfere;
but you shall do as you will with your own world. I will give you men in
abundance, for I will make great minds and vast, whom you shall call lords
of earth; you shall have orators, you shall have philosophers. Find Me out, O
reason, find Me out, O wisdom; discover My nature, if you can: find Me out
unto perfection, if you are able; and if you cannot, then shut your mouth forever, and then I will teach you that the wisdom of God is wiser than the
wisdom of man; yea, that the foolishness of God is wiser than men."

And how did the reason of man work out the problem? How did wis-

* This sermon was preached on Sunday morning, February 11, 1855, at Exeter
Hall, Strand, and is reprinted from *The New Park Street Pulpit*.

dom perform her feat? Look upon the heathen nations; there you see the result of wisdom's researches. In the time of Jesus Christ, you might have beheld the earth covered with the slime of pollution—a Sodom on a large scale—corrupt, filthy, depraved, indulging in vices which we dare not mention, reveling in lusts too abominable even for our imagination to dwell upon for a moment. We find the men prostrating themselves before blocks of wood and stone, adoring ten thousand gods more vicious than themselves. We find, in fact, that reason wrote out her own depravity with a finger covered with blood and filth, and that she forever cut herself out from all her glory, by the vile deeds she did. She would not worship God. She would not bow down to Him who is "clearly seen," but she worshiped any creature: the reptile that crawled, the crocodile, the viper, everything might be a god, but not, forsooth, the God of heaven. Vice might be made into a ceremony; the greatest crime might be exalted into a religion; but of true worship she knew nothing.

Poor reason! poor wisdom! how you have fallen from heaven! Like Lucifer—son of the morning—you are lost. You have written out your conclusion, but it is a conclusion of consummate folly. "After that in the wisdom of God the world by wisdom knew not God, it pleased God by the foolishness of preaching to save them that believe."

Wisdom had had its time, and time enough; it had done its all, and that was little enough; it had made the world worse than it was before it stepped upon it, and now, says God, "Foolishness shall overcome wisdom; now ignorance, as you call it, shall sweep away your science; now, humble, child-like faith, shall crumble to the dust all the colossal systems your hands have piled." He calls His army. Christ puts His trumpet to His mouth, and up come the warriors, clad in fisherman's garb, with the brogue of the lake of Galilee—poor humble mariners. Here are the warriors, O wisdom! that are to confound you; these are the heroes who shall overcome your proud philosophers! These men are to plant their standard upon the ruined walls of your strongholds, and bid them fall forever; these men, and their successors, are to exalt a gospel in the world which you may laugh at as absurd, which you may sneer at as folly, but which shall be exalted above the hills, and shall be glorious even to the highest heavens.

Since that day, God has always raised up successors of the apostles. I claim to be a successor of the apostles, not by any lineal descent, but because I have the same roll and charter as any apostle, and am as much called to preach the gospel as Paul himself: if not as much owned in the conversion of sinners, yet in a measure, blessed of God; and, therefore, here I stand, foolish as Paul might be, foolish as Peter, or any of those fisherman, but still with the might of God I grasp the sword of truth—coming here to "preach Christ and him crucified, unto the Jews a stumblingblock, and unto the Greeks foolishness; but unto them which are called, both Jews and unto the Greeks foolishness; but unto them which are called, both Jews and Greeks, Christ the power of God and the wisdom of God."

Before I enter upon our text, let me briefly tell you what I believe preaching Christ and Him crucified is. My friends, I do not believe it is preaching Christ and Him crucified, to give our people a batch of philosophy every Sunday morning and evening, and neglect the truth of this Holy Book. I do not believe it is preaching Christ and Him crucified, to leave out the main cardinal doctrines of the Word of God, and preach a religion which is all a mist and a haze, without any definite truths whatever. I take it *that* man does not preach Christ and Him crucified, who can get through a sermon without mentioning Christ's name once; nor does that man preach Christ and Him crucified who leaves out the Holy Spirit's work, who never says a word about the Holy Spirit, so that indeed the hearers might say, "We do not so much as know whether there be a Holy Spirit."

And I have my own private opinion that there is no such thing as preaching Christ and Him crucified, unless you preach what nowadays is called Calvinism. I have my own ideas, and those I always state boldly. It is a nickname to call it Calvinism; Calvinism is the gospel, and nothing else. I do not believe we can preach the gospel, if we do not preach justification by faith, without works; nor unless we exalt the electing, unchangeable, eternal, immutable, conquering, love of Jehovah; nor do I think we can preach the gospel, unless we base it upon the peculiar redemption which Christ made for His elect and chosen people; nor can I comprehend a gospel which lets saints fall away after they are called, and suffers the children of God to be burned in the fires of damnation after having believed. Such a gospel I abhor. The gospel of the Bible is not such a gospel as that. We preach Christ and Him crucified in a different fashion, and to all gainsayers we reply, "We have not so learned Christ."

There are three things in the text. First, a gospel rejected—"Christ, crucified, to the Jews a sumblingblock, and to the Greeks foolishness"; secondly, a gospel triumphant—"unto those which are called, both Jews and Greeks"; and thirdly, a gospel admired—it is to them who are called "the power of God; and the wisdom of God."

A Gospel Rejected

First, we have here A GOSPEL REJECTED. One would have imagined that when God sent His gospel, all people would meekly listen, and humbly receive its truths. We should have thought that God's ministers had but to proclaim that life is brought to light by the gospel, and that Christ is come to save sinners, and every ear would be attentive, every eye would be fixed, and every heart would be wide open to receive the truth. We should have said, judging favorably of our fellow-creatures, that there would not exist in the world a monster so vile, so depraved, so polluted, as to put so much as a stone in the way of the progress of truth; we could not have conceived such a thing; yet that conception is the truth.

When the gospel was preached, instead of being accepted and admired, one universal hiss went up to heaven; men could not bear it; its first Preacher they dragged to the brow of the hill, and would have sent Him down headlong: yea, they did more, they nailed Him to the cross, and there they let Him languish out His dying life in agony such as no man has borne since. All His chosen ministers have been hated and abhorred by worldlings; instead of being listened to, they have been scoffed at—treated as if they were the offscouring of all things, and the very scum of mankind. Look at the holy men in the old times, how they were driven from city to city, persecuted, afflicted, tormented, stoned to death wherever the enemy had power to do so. Those friends of men, those real philanthropists, who came with hearts big with love, and hands full of mercy, and lips pregnant with celestial fire, and souls that burned with holy influence; those men were treated as if they were spies in the camp, as if they were deserters from the common cause of mankind; as if they were enemies, and not, as they truly were, the best of friends.

Do not suppose, my friends, that men like the gospel any better now than they did then. There is an idea that you are growing better. I do not believe it. You are growing worse. In many respects men may be better—outwardly better—but the heart within is still the same. The human heart of today dissected would be just like the human heart a thousand years ago; the gall of bitterness within that breast of yours is just as bitter as the gall of bitterness in that of Simon of old. We have in our hearts the same latent opposition to the truth of God; and hence we find men even as of old, who scorn the gospel.

I shall, in speaking of the gospel rejected, endeavor to point out the two classes of persons who equally despise the truth. The Jews make it a stumbling block, and the Greeks account it foolishness. Now these two very respectable gentlemen—the Jew and the Greek—I am not going to make these ancient individuals the object of my condemnation, but I look upon them as members of a great parliament, representatives of a great constituency, and I shall attempt to show that if all the race of Jews were cut off, there would be still a great number in the world who would answer to the name of Jews, to whom Christ is a stumbling block; and that if Greece were swallowed up by some earthquake, and ceased to be a nation, there would still be the Greek unto whom the gospel would be foolishness. I shall simply introduce the Jew and the Greek, and let them speak a moment to you, in order that you may see the gentlemen who represent you; the representative men; the persons who stand for many of you, who as yet are not called by divine grace.

The first is the Jew; to him the gospel is a stumbling block. A respectable man the Jew was in his day; all formal religion was concentrated in his person; he went up to the temple very devoutly; he tithed all he had, even to the mint and the cummin. You would see him fasting twice in the week, with a face all marked with sadness and sorrow. If you looked at him, he had the law between his eyes; there was the phylactery, and the borders of his garments of amazing width, that he might never be supposed to be a Gentile dog; that no one might ever conceive that he was not a Hebrew of pure descent. He had a holy ancestry; he came of a pious family; a right good man was he. He could not endure those Sadducees at all, who had no religion. He was thoroughly a religious man; he stood up for his synagogue; he would not have that temple on Mount Gerizim; he could not bear the Samaritans, he had no dealings with them; he was a religionist of the first order, a man of the very finest kind; a specimen of a man who is a moralist, and who loves the ceremonies of the law.

Accordingly, when he heard about Christ, he asked who Christ was. "The son of a carpenter." "Ah!" "The son of a carpenter, and His mother's name was Mary, and His father's name Joseph." "That of itself is presumption enough," said he, "positive proof, in fact, that He cannot be the Messiah. And what does He say?" "Why He says, 'Woe unto you, Scribes and Pharisees, hypocrites.'" "That won't do." "Moreover," He says, "'It is not by the works of the flesh that any man can enter into the kingdom of heaven.'" The Jew tied a double knot in his phylactery at once; he thought he would have the borders of his garment made twice as broad. *He* bow to the Nazarene! No, no; and if so much as a disciple crossed the street, he thought the place polluted, and would not tread in his steps. Do you think he would give up his old father's religion—the religion which came from Mount Sinai—that old religion that lay in the ark and the overshadowing cherubim? He give that up? not he. A vile impostor—that is all Christ was in his eyes. So he thought.

Accordingly, he turned a deaf ear to all the Preacher's eloquence and listened not at all. Farewell, old Jew. You sleep with your fathers, and your generation is a wandering race, still walking the earth. Farewell, I have done with you. Alas! poor wretch, that Christ who was your stumbling block, shall be your Judge, and on your head shall be that loud curse: "His blood be on us and on our children." But I am going to find out Mr. Jew here in Exeter Hall—persons who answer to his description—to whom Jesus Christ is a stumbling block. Let me introduce you to yourselves, some of you. You were of a pious family too, were you not? Yes. And you have a religion which you love—you love it so far as the chrysalis of it goes, the outside, the covering, the husk. You would not have one rubric altered, nor one of those dear old arches taken down, nor the stained glass removed from all the world; and any man who should say a word against such things, you would set down as a heretic at once. Or, perhaps you do not go to such a place of worship, but you love some plain old meeting-house, where your forefathers worshiped, called a dissenting chapel. Ah! it is a beautiful plain place; you love it, you love its ordinances, you love its exterior; and if anyone spoke against the place, how vexed you would feel. You think that what they do there, they ought to do everywhere; in fact your church is a model one; the place where you go, is exactly the sort of place for everybody; and if I were to ask you why you hope to go to heaven, you would, perhaps, say, "Because I am a Baptist," or, "Because I am an Episcopalian," or whatever other sect you belong to.

There is yourself; I know Jesus Christ will be to you a stumbling block. If I come and tell you that all your going to the house of God is good for nothing; if I tell you that all those many times you have been singing and praying, all pass for nothing in the sight of God, because you are a hyp-ocrite and a formalist. If I tell you that your heart is not right with God, and that unless it is so, all the external is good for nothing, I know what you will say—"I shan't hear that young man again." It is a stumbling block. If you had stepped in anywhere where you had heard formalism exalted; if you had been told "this must you do, and this other must you do, and then you will be saved," you would highly approve of it. But how many are there externally religious, with whose characters you could find no fault, but who have never had the regenerating influence of the Holy Spirit; who never were made to lie prostrate on their face before Calvary's cross; who never turned a wishful eye to yonder Savior crucified; who never put their trust in the One who was slain for the sons of men. They love a superficial religion, but when a man talks deeper than that, they set it down for cant.

You may love all that is external about religion, just as you may love a man for his clothes—caring nothing for the man himself. If so, I know you are one of those who reject the gospel. You will hear me preach; and while I speak about the externals, you will hear me with attention; while I plead for morality, and argue against drunkenness, or show the heinous-ness of Sabbath-breaking, all well and good; but if once I say, "Except ye be converted, and become as little children, ye can in no wise enter into the kingdom of God"; if once I tell you that you must be elected of God—that you must be purchased with the Savior's blood—that you must be con-verted by the Holy Spirit—you say, "He is a fanatic! Away with him, away with him! We do not want to hear that anymore." Christ crucified is to the Jew—the ceremonialist—a stumbling block.

But there is another specimen of this Jew to be found. He is thoroughly orthodox in his sentiments. As for forms and ceremonies, he thinks noth-ing about them. He goes to a place of worship where he learns sound doctrine. He will hear nothing but what is true. He likes that we should have good works and morality. He is a good man, and no man can find fault with him. Here he is, regular in his Sunday pew. In the market he walks before men in all honesty—so you would imagine. Ask him about any doctrine, and he can give you a disquisition upon it. In fact, he could write a treatise upon anything in the Bible, and a great many things besides. He knows almost everything; and here, up in this dark attic of the head, his religion has taken up its abode; he has a best parlor down in his heart, but his religion never goes there—that is shut against it. He has money in there—mammon, worldliness; or he has something else—self-love, pride. Perhaps he loves to hear experimental preaching; he admires it all; in fact, he loves anything that is sound. But then he has not any sound in himself: or rather, it is all sound and there is no substance. He likes to hear true doctrine; but it never penetrates his inner man.

You never see him weep. Preach to him about Christ crucified, a glorious subject, and you never see a tear roll down his cheek; tell him of the mighty influence of the Holy Spirit—he admires you for it, but he never had the hand of the Holy Spirit on his soul; tell him about communion with God, plunging into Godhead's deepest sea, and being lost in its immensity—the man loves to hear, but he never experiences, he has never communed with Christ; and accordingly when once you begin to strike home, when you lay him on the table, take out your dissecting knife, begin to cut him up, and show him his own heart, let him see what it is by nature, and what it must become by grace—the man starts, he cannot stand that; he wants none of that—Christ received in the heart and accepted.

Albeit, that he loves it enough in the head, 'tis to him a stumbling block, and he casts it away. Do you see yourselves here, my friends? See yourselves as others see you? See yourselves as God sees you? For so it is, here be many to whom Christ is as much a stumbling block now as ever He was. O formalists! I speak to you; O you who have the nutshell, but abhor the kernel; O you who like the trappings and the dress, but care not for that fair virgin who is clothed therewith: O you who admire the paint and the tinsel, but abhor the solid gold, I speak to you; I ask you, does your religion give you solid comfort? Can you stare death in the face with it, and say, "I know that my Redeemer liveth"? Can you close your eyes at night, singing as your vesper song—

> I to the end must endure,
> As sure as the earnest is given?

Can you bless God for affliction? Can you plunge in dressed as you are, and swim through all the floods of trial? Can you march triumphant through the lion's den, laugh at affliction, and bid defiance to hell? Can you? No! Your gospel is an effeminate thing; a thing of words and sounds, and not of power. Cast it from you, I beseech you: it is not worth your keeping; and when you come before the throne of God, you will find it will fail you, and fail you so that you shall never find another; for lost, ruined, destroyed, you shall find that Christ who is "a stumbling block," will be your Judge.

I have found out the Jew, and I have now to discover the Greek. He is a person of quite a different exterior to the Jew. As to the phylactery, to him it is all rubbish; and as to the broad-hemmed garment, he despises it. He does not care for the forms of religion; he has an intense aversion, in fact, to broad-brimmed hats, or to everything which looks like outward show. He appreciates eloquence; he admires a smart saying; he loves a quaint expression; he likes to read the last new book; he is a Greek, and to him the gospel is foolishness.

The Greek is a gentleman found in most places nowadays: manufactured sometimes in colleges, constantly made in schools, produced everywhere. He is on the exchange; in the market; he keeps a shop; rides in a carriage; he is a noble, a gentleman; he is everywhere; even in court. He is thoroughly wise. Ask him anything, and he knows it. Ask for a quotation from any of the old poets, or anyone else, and he can give it you. If you are a Mahommedan, and plead the claims of our religion, he will hear you very patiently. But if you are a Christian, and talk to him of Jesus Christ, "Stop your cant," he says, "I don't want to hear anything about that."

This Grecian gentleman believes all philosophy except the true one; he studies all wisdom except the wisdom of God; he seeks all learning except spiritual learning; he loves everything except that which God approves; he likes everything which man makes, and nothing which comes from God; it is foolishness to him, confounded foolishness. You have only to discourse about one doctrine in the Bible, and he shuts his ears; he wishes no longer for your company; it is foolishness.

I have met this gentleman a great many times. Once when I saw him, he told me he did not believe in any religion at all; and when I said I did, and had a hope that when I died I should go to heaven, he said he dared say it was very comfortable, but he did not believe in religion, and that he was sure it was best to live as nature dictated. Another time he spoke well of all religions, and believed they were very good in their place, and all true; and he had no doubt that if a man were sincere in any kind of religion, he would be all right at last. I told him I did not think so, and that I believed there was but one religion revealed of God—the religion of God's elect, the religion which is the gift of Jesus. He then said I was a bigot, and wished me good morning. It was to him foolishness.

He had nothing to do with me at all. He either liked no religion, or every religion. Another time I held him by the coat button, and I discussed with him a little about faith. He said, "It is all very well, I believe that is true Protestant doctrine." But presently I said something about election, and he said, "I don't like that; many people have preached that and turned it to bad account." I then hinted something about free grace; but that he could not endure, it was to him foolishness. He was a polished Greek, and thought that if he were not chosen, he ought to be. He never liked that passage— "Gad hath chosen the foolish things of this world to confound the wise, and the things which are not, to bring to nought things that are." He thought it was very discreditable to the Bible; and when the book was revised, he had no doubt it would be cut out.

To such a man—for he is here today, very likely come to hear this reed shaken of the wind—I have to say this: Ah! wise man, full of worldly wisdom; your wisdom will stand you here, but what will you do in the swellings of Jordan? Philosophy may do well for you to lean upon while you walk through this world; but the river is deep, and you will want something more than that. If you have not the arm of the Most High to hold you up in the flood and cheer you with promises, you will sink; with all your philosophy, you will sink; with all your learning, you shall sink, and be washed into that awful ocean of eternal torment, where you shall be forever. Ah! Greeks, it may be foolishness to you, but you shall see the Man your Judge, and then you shall rue the day that you ever said God's gospel was foolishness.

The Gospel Triumphant

Having spoken thus far upon the gospel rejected, I shall now briefly speak upon THE GOSPEL TRIUMPHANT. "Unto us who are called, both Jews and Greeks, it is the power of God, and the wisdom of God." Yonder man rejects the gospel, despises grace, and laughs at it as a delusion. Here is another man who laughed at it too; but God will fetch him down upon his knees. Christ shall not die for nothing. The Holy Spirit shall not strive in vain. God has said, "My word shall not return unto me void, but it shall accomplish that which I please, and it shall prosper in the thing whereto I sent it." "He shall see of the travail of his soul, and shall be abundantly satisfied." If one sinner is not saved, another shall be. The Jew and the Greek shall never depopulate heaven. The choirs of glory shall not lose a single songster by all the opposition of Jews and Greeks; for God has said it; some shall be called; some shall be saved; some shall be rescued.

> Perish the virtue, as it ought, abhorred,
> And the fool with it, who insults his Lord.
> The atonement a Redeemer's love has wrought
> Is not for you—the righteous need it not.
> Seest thou yon harlot wooing all she meets,
> The worn-out nuisance of the public streets,
> Herself from morn to night, from night to morn,
> Her own abhorrence, and as much your scorn:
> The gracious shower, unlimited and free,

> Shall fall on her when heaven denies it thee.
> Of all that wisdom dictate, this the drift,
> That man is dead in sin, and life a gift.

If the righteous and good are not saved, if they reject the gospel, there are others who are to be called, others who shall be rescued, for Christ will not lose the merits of His agonies, or the purchase of His blood.

"Unto us who are called." I received a note this week asking me to explain that word *"called"*; because in one passage it says, "Many are called but few are chosen," while in another it appears that all who are called must be chosen. Now, let me observe that there are two calls. As my old friend John Bunyan says, "The hen has two calls, the common cluck, which she gives daily and hourly, and the special one which she means for her little chickens." So there is a general call, a call made to every man; every man hears it. Many are called by it; you are all called this morning in that sense; but very few are chosen. The other is a special call, the children's call. You know how the bell sounds over the workshop to call the men to work—that is a general call. A father goes to the door and calls out, "John, it is dinner-time"—that is the special call. Many are called with the general call, but they are not chosen; the special call is for the children only, and that is what is meant in the text, "Unto us who are called, both Jews and Greeks, Christ the power of God and the wisdom of God."

That call is always a special one. While I stand here and call men, nobody comes; while I preach to sinners universally, no good is done; it is like the sheet lightning you sometimes see on the summer's evening, beautiful, grand, but who have ever heard of anything being struck by it? But the special call is the forked flash from heaven; it strikes somewhere; it is the arrow sent in between the joints of the harness. The call which saves is like that of Jesus, when He said, "Mary," and she said unto Him, "Rabboni." Do you know anything about that special call, my beloved? Did Jesus ever call you by name? Can you recollect the hour when He whispered your name in your ear, when He said, "Come to me"?

If so, you will grant the truth of what I am going to say next about it— that it is an effectual call. There is no resisting it. When God calls with His special call, there is no standing out. Ah! I know I laughed at religion; I despised, I abhorred it; but that call! Oh! I would not come. But God said, "You shall come. All that the Father gives Me shall come." "Lord, I will not." "But you shall," said God.

And I have gone up to God's house sometimes almost with a resolution that I would not listen, but listen I must. Oh! how the Word came into my soul! Was there a power of resistance? No; I was thrown down; each bone seemed to be broken; I was saved by effectual grace. I appeal to your experience, my friends. When God took you in hand, could you withstand Him?

You stood against your minister times enough. Sickness did not break you down; disease did not bring you to God's feet; eloquence did not convince you; but when God put His hand to the work, ah! then what change; like Saul, with his horses going to Damascus, that voice from heaven said, "I am Jesus whom thou persecutest. Saul, Saul, why persecutest thou me?" There was no going further then. That was an effectual call.

Like that, again, which Jesus gave to Zaccheus, when he was up in the tree: stepping under the tree, He said, "Zaccheus, come down, today I must abide at your house." Zaccheus was taken in the net; he heard his own name; the call sank into his soul; he could not stop up in the tree, for an Almighty impulse drew him down. And I could tell you some singular instances of persons going to the house of God and having their characters described, limned out to perfection, so that they have said, "He is painting me, He is painting me." Just as I might say to that young man here who stole his master's gloves yesterday, that Jesus calls him to repentance. It may be that there is such a person here; and when the call comes to a peculiar character, it generally comes with a special power. God gives His ministers a brush, and shows them how to use it in painting lifelike portraits, and thus the sinner hears the special call. I cannot give the special call; God alone can give it, and I leave it with Him. Some must be called. Jew and Greek may laugh, but still there are some who are called, both Jews and Greeks.

Then to close up this second point, it is a great mercy that many a Jew has been made to drop his self-righteousness; many a legalist has been made to drop his legalism and come to Christ; many a Greek has bowed his genius at the throne of God's gospel. We have a few such. As Cowper says:

> We boast some rich ones whom the gospel sways,
> And one who wears a coronet and prays;
> Like gleamings of an olive tree they show,
> Here and there one upon the topmost bough.

A Gospel Admired

Now we come to our third point, A GOSPEL ADMIRED. Unto us who are called of God, it is the power of God, and the wisdom of God. Now, beloved, this must be a matter of pure experience between your souls and God. If you are called of God this morning, you will know it. I know there are times when a Christian has to say,

> Tis a point I long to know,
>   Oft it causes anxious thought;
> Do I love the Lord or no?
>   Am I His, or am I not?

But if a man never in his life knew himself to be a Christian, he never was a Christian. If he never had a moment of confidence, when he could say, "Now I know in whom I have believed," I think I do not utter a harsh thing when I say, that man could not have been born again; for I do not understand how a man can be killed and then made alive again, and not know it; how a man can pass from death unto life, and not know it; how a man can be brought out of darkness into marvelous light without knowing it. I am sure I know it, when I shout out my old verse,

> Now free from sin, I walk at large,
> My Savior's blood's my full discharge;
> At His dear feet content I lay,
> A sinner saved, and homage pay.

There are moments when the eyes glisten with joy; and we can say, "We are persuaded, confident, certain." I do not wish to distress anyone who is under doubt. Often gloomy doubts will prevail; there are seasons when you fear you have not been called; when you doubt your interest in Christ. Ah! what a mercy it is that it is not your hold of Christ that saves you, but His hold of you! What a sweet fact that it is not how you grasp His hand, but His grasp of yours, that saves you. Yet I think you ought to know sometime or other, whether you are called of God. If so, you will follow me in the next part of my discourse which is a matter of pure experience; unto us who are saved, it is "Christ the power of God, and the wisdom of God."

The gospel is to the true believer a thing of power. It is Christ the power of God. Aye, there is a power in God's gospel beyond all description. Once, I, like Mazeppa, bound on the wild horse of my lust, bound hand and foot, inescapable of resistance, was galloping on with hell's wolves behind me, howling for my body and my soul, as their just and lawful prey. There came a mighty hand which stopped that wild horse, cut my bands, set me down, and brought me into liberty.

Is there power, sir? Aye, there is power, and he who has felt it must acknowledge it. There was a time when I lived in the strong old castle of my sins, and rested in my works. There came a trumpeter to the door, and bade me open it. I with anger chide him from the porch, and said he never should enter. There came a goodly personage, with loving countenance; His hands were marked with scars, where nails were driven, and His feet had nail-prints too; He lifted up His cross, using it as a hammer; at the first blow the gate of my prejudice shook; at the second it trembled more; at the third down it fell, and in He came; and He said, "Arise, and stand upon your feet, for I have loved you with an everlasting love." A thing of power! Ah! it is a thing of power. I have felt it *here*, in this heart; I have the witness of the Spirit within, and know it is a thing of might, because it has conquered me; it has bowed me down.

> His free grace alone, from the first to the last,
> Hath won my affection, and held my soul fast.

To the Christian the gospel is a thing of power. What is it that makes the young man devote himself as a missionary to the cause of God, to leave father and mother, and go into distant lands? It is a thing of power that does it—it is the gospel. What is it that constrains yonder minister, in the midst of the cholera, to climb up that creaking staircase, and stand by the bed of some dying creature who has that dire disease? It must be a thing of power which leads him to risk his life; it is love of the cross of Christ which bids him do it. What is that which enables one man to stand up before a multitude of his fellows, all unprepared it may be, but determined that he will speak nothing but Christ and Him crucified? What is it that enables him to cry, like the war-horse of Job in battle, Aha! and move glorious in might?

It is a thing of power that does it—it is Christ crucified. And what emboldens that timid female to walk down that dark lane in the wet evening, that she may go and sit beside the victim of a contagious fever? What strengthens her to go through that den of thieves, and pass by the profligate and profane? What influences her to enter into that charnel-house of death, and there sit down and whisper words of comfort? Does gold make her do it? They are too poor to give her gold. Does fame make her do it? She shall never be known, nor written among the mighty women of this earth. What makes her do it? Is it love of merit? No; she knows she has no desert before high heaven. What impels her to it? It is the power of the gospel on her heart; it is the cross of Christ; she loves it, and she therefore says—

> Were the whole realm of nature mine.
> That were a present far too small;
> Love so amazing, so divine,
> Demands my soul, my life, my all.

But I behold another scene. A martyr is hurried to the stake; the soldiers are around him; the crowds are mocking, but he is marching steadily on. See, they bind him, with a chain around his middle, to the stake; they heap faggots all about him; the flame is lighted up; listen to his words; "Bless the Lord, O my soul, and all that is within me, bless His holy name." The flames are kindling round his legs; the fire is burning him even to the bone; see him lift up his hands, and say, "I know that my Redeemer liveth, and though the fire devour this body, yet in my flesh shall I see the Lord." Behold him clutch the stake, and kiss it as if he loved it, and hear him say, "For every chain of iron that man girds me with, God shall give me a chain of gold, for all these faggots, and this ignominy and shame, He shall increase the weight of my eternal glory." See, all the under parts of his body are consumed; still he lives in the torture; at last he bows himself, and the upper part of his body falls over; and as he falls you hear him say, "Into thy hands I commend my spirit."

What wondrous magic was on him, sirs? What made that man strong? What helped him to bear that cruelty? What made him stand unmoved in the flames? It was the thing of power; it was the cross of Jesus crucified. For "unto us who are saved it is the power of God."

But behold another scene far different. There is no crowd there; it is a silent room. There is a poor pallet, a lonely bed: a physician standing by. There is a young girl; her face is blanched by consumption; the worm has eaten her cheek, and though sometimes the flush came, it was the death-flush of the deceitful destroyer. There she lies, weak, pale, wan, worn, dying: yet behold a smile in her voice. Joan of Arc of old was not half so mighty as that girl. She is wrestling with dragons on her deathbed; but see her composure, and hear her dying sonnet:

> Jesus! lover of my soul,
>   Let me to Thy bosom fly,
> While the billows near me roll,—
>   While the tempest still is high!
>
> Hide me, O my Savior! hide
>   Till the storm of life is past!
> Safe into the haven guide;
>   O, receive my soul at last!

And with a smile she shuts her eye on earth, and opens it in heaven. What enables her to die like that? It is the power of God unto salvation; it is the cross; it is Jesus crucified.

I have little time to discourse upon the other point, and be it far from me to weary you by a lengthened and prosy sermon, but we must glance at the other statement: Christ is, to the called ones, the wisdom of God, as well as the power of God. To a believer, the gospel is the perfection of wisdom, and if it appear not so to the ungodly, it is because of the perversion of judgment consequent on their depravity.

An idea has long possessed the public mind—that a religious man can scarcely be a wise man. It has been the custom to talk of infidels, atheists, and deists, as men of deep thought and comprehensive intellect; and to tremble for the Christian controversialist, as if he must surely fall by the hand of his enemy. But this is purely a mistake; for the gospel is the sum of wisdom; an epitome of knowledge; a treasure-house of truth; and a revelation of mysterious secrets. In it we see how justice and mercy may be married; here we behold inexorable law entirely satisfied, and sovereign love bearing away the sinner in triumph. Our meditation upon it enlarges the mind; and as it opens to our soul in successive flashes of glory, we stand astonished at the profound wisdom manifest in it.

Ah, dear friends! if you seek wisdom, you shall see it displayed in all its greatness; not in the balancing of the clouds, nor the firmness of earth's foundations; not in the measured march of the armies of the sky, nor in the perpetual motion of the waves of the sea; not in vegetation with all its fairy forms of beauty; nor in the animal with its marvelous tissue of nerve, and vein, and sinew: nor even in man, that last and loftiest work of the Creator. But turn aside and see this great sight!—an incarnate God upon the cross; a substitute atoning for mortal guilt; a sacrifice satisfying the vengeance of heaven; and delivering the rebellious sinner. Here is essential wisdom; enthroned, crowned, glorified. Admire you men of earth, if you be not blind: and you, who glory in your learning, bend your hearts in reverence, and own that all your skill could not have devised a gospel at once so just to God, so safe to man.

Remember, my friends, that while the gospel is in itself wisdom, it also confers wisdom on its students; she teaches young men wisdom and discretion, and gives understanding to the simple. A man who is a believing admirer and a hearty lover of the truth, as it is in Jesus, is in a right place to follow with advantage any other branch of science.

I confess I have a shelf in my head for everything now. Whatever I read I know where to put it; whatever I learn I know where to stow it away. Once when I read books, I put all my knowledge together in glorious confusion; but ever since I have known Christ, I have put Christ in the center as my sun, and each science revolves round it like a planet, while minor sciences are satellites to these planets. Christ is to me the wisdom of God. I can learn everything now. The science of Christ crucified is the most excellent of sciences, she is to me the wisdom of God. O, young man, build your studio on Calvary! There raise your observatory, and scan by faith the lofty things of nature. Take a hermit's cell in the garden of Gethsemane, and wash your brow with the waters of Siloa. Let the Bible be your standard classic—your last appeal in matters of contention. Let its light be your illumination, and you shall become more wise than Plato; more truly learned than the seven sages of antiquity.

And now, my dear friends, solemnly and earnestly, as in the sight of God, I appeal to you. You are gathered here, I know, from different motives; some of you have come from curiosity; others of you are my regular hearers; some have come from one place and some from another. What have you heard me say? I have told you of two classes of persons who reject Christ; the *religionist* who has a religion of form and nothing else; and the *man of the world* who calls our gospel foolishness. Now put your hand upon your heart and ask yourself, "Am I one of these?" If you are, then walk the earth in all your pride; then go as you came in; but know that for all this the Lord shall bring you into judgment; know that your joys and delights shall vanish like a dream, "and, like the baseless fabric of a vision," be swept away forever. Know this, moreover, O man, that one day in the halls of Satan, down in hell, I perhaps may see you amongst those myriad spirits who revolve forever in a perpetual circle with their hands upon their hearts. If your hand be transparent, and your flesh transparent, I shall look through your hand and flesh, and see your heart within. And how shall I see it? Set in a case of fire—in a case of fire! And there you shall revolve forever, with the worm gnawing within your heart, which shall never die—a case of fire around your never-dying, ever tortured heart. Good God! let not these men still reject and despise Christ; but let this be the time when they shall be called.

To the rest of you who are called, I need say nothing. The longer you live, the more powerful will you find the gospel to be; the more deeply Christ-taught you are, the more you live under the constant influence of the Holy Spirit, the more you will know the gospel to be a thing of power, and the more also will you understand it to be a thing of wisdom. May every blessing rest upon you; and may God come up with us in the evening!

> Let men or angels dig the mines
> Where nature's golden treasure shines;
> Brought near the doctrine of the cross,
> All nature's gold appears but dross.
>
> Should vile blasphemers with disdain
> Pronounce the truths of Jesus vain,
> We'll meet the scandal and the shame,
> And sing and triumph in His name.

6

*Christ Crucified**

For I determined not to know any thing among you, save Jesus Christ, and him crucified (1 Corinthians 2:2).

Corinth was situated in the midst of a people who admired eloquence and wisdom. This Epistle was written in the age of orators and philosophers. The apostle Paul was a man of profound learning; he had been educated at the feet of Gamaliel in all the wisdom of the East. We are quite sure he was a man of a very capacious mind; for, although his writings were inspired by the Holy Spirit, yet the Holy Spirit chose as His instrument a man evidently possessing the capacity for strong and vigorous thought and argument; and as for his oratorical powers, I believe that, if he had chosen to cultivate them, they would have been of the very first order, for we have in some of his Epistles eloquence more sublime than ever fell from the lips of Cicero or Demosthenes.

The temptation would exist, in the mind of any ordinary man entering into such a city as Corinth, to say within himself, "I will endeavor to excel in all the graces of oratory; I have a blessed gospel to preach that is worthy of the highest talents that ever can be consecrated to it." "I am," Paul might have said to himself, "largely gifted in the matter of eloquence, I must now endeavor carefully to polish my rhetoric, and so to fashion my address as to excel all the orators who now attract the Corinthians to listen to them. This I may do very laudably, for I will still keep in view my intention of preaching Jesus Christ; and I will preach Jesus Christ with such a flow of noble language that I shall be able to win my audience to consider the subject."

But the apostle resolved to do no such thing. "No," said he, "before I enter the gates of Corinth, this is my firm determination; if any good is to be done there, if any are led to believe in Christ the Messiah, their belief

---

* This sermon was intended for reading on Sunday, May 6, 1900, and was preached at New Park Street Chapel, Southwark, on a Sunday evening, early in the year 1858. It is taken from *The Metropolitan Tabernacle Pulpit.*

72

shall be the result of hearing the gospel, and not of my eloquence. It shall never be said, 'Oh! no wonder that Christianity spreads, see what an able advocate it has'; but it shall be said, 'How mighty must be the grace of God which has convinced these persons by such simple preaching, and brought them to know the Lord Jesus Christ by such humble instrumentality as that of the apostle Paul!'" He resolved to put a curb upon his fiery tongue, he determined that he would be slow in speech in the midst of them; and, instead of magnifying himself, he would magnify his office, and magnify the grace of God by denying himself the full use of those powers, which, had they been dedicated to God—as indeed they were—but had they been fully employed, as some would have used them, might have achieved for him the reputation of being the most eloquent preacher upon the face of the earth.

Again, he might have said, "These philosophers are very wise men; if I would be a match for them, I must be very wise, too. These Corinthians are a very noble race of people; they have been for a long time under the tuition of these talented men. I must speak as they speak, in enigmas and with many sophisms; I must always be propounding some dark problem. I need not live in the tub of Diogenes; but if I take his lantern, I may do something with it; I must try and borrow some of his wisdom. I have a profound philosophy to preach to these clever people; and if I liked to preach that philosophy, I should dash in pieces all their theories concerning mental and moral science. I have found out a wondrous secret, and I might stand in the midst of the marketplace, and cry, 'Eureka, Eureka,' 'I have found it,' but I do not care to build my gospel upon the foundation of human wisdom. No, if any are brought to believe in Christ, it shall be from the simple unadorned gospel, plainly preached in unpolished language. The faith of my hearers, if they are converted to God, shall not stand in the wisdom of men, but in the power of God."

Can you not see, dear friends, that the apostle had very good reasons for coming to this determination? When a man says that he is determined to do a certain thing, it looks as if he knew that it was a difficult thing to do. So, it must have been a hard thing for the apostle to determine to keep to this one subject, "Jesus Christ, and Him crucified." I am sure that nine-tenths of the ministers of this age could not have done it. Fancy Paul going through the streets of Corinth, and hearing a philosopher explain the current theory of creation. He is telling the people something about the world springing out of certain things that previously existed, and the apostle Paul thinks, "I could easily correct that man's mistakes; I could tell him that the Lord created all things in six days, and rested on the seventh, and show him in the Book of Genesis the inspired account of the creation." "But, no," he says to himself, "I have a more important message than that to deliver."

Still, he must have felt as if he would have liked to set him right; for, you know, when you hear a man uttering a gross falsehood, you feel as if you would like to go in, and do battle with him. But instead of that, the apostle just thinks, *It is not my business to set the people right about their theory of the creation of the world. All that I have to do is to know nothing but Jesus Christ, and Him crucified.*

Besides, in Corinth, there was now and then sure to be a political struggle, and I have no doubt that the apostle Paul felt for his people, the Jews, and he would have liked to see all his Jewish kindred have the privilege of citizenship. Sometimes the Corinthians would hold a public meeting, in which they would support the opinion that the Jews ought not to have citizenship in Corinth; might not the apostle have made a speech at such a gathering? If he had been asked to do so, he would have said, "I know nothing about such matters; all I know is Jesus Christ, and Him crucified."

They had political lectures, no doubt, in Corinth; and one man delivered a lecture upon this subject, and another upon that; in fact, all kinds of wonderful themes taken from the ancient poets were descanted upon by different men. Did not the apostle Paul take one of the lectures? Did he not say, "I may throw a little gospel into it, and so do some good"? No, he said, "I come here as Christ's minister, and I will never be anything else but Christ's minister; I will never address the Corinthians in any other character than that of Christ's ambassador. For one thing only have I determined to know, and that is Jesus Christ, and Him crucified." Would to God that all the ministers of this age had determined to do the same!

Do you not sometimes find a minister who takes a prominent part in an election, who thinks it his business to stand forth on the political platform of the nation; and did it ever strike you that he was out of his place, that it was his business to know nothing among men save Jesus Christ, and Him crucified? Do we not see, at every corner of our streets, a lecture advertised to be delivered on this and that and the other subject, by this minister and that, who leave their pulpits in order that they may be enabled to deliver lectures upon all kinds of subjects? "No," Paul would have said, "if I cannot spread the gospel of Christ legitimately, by preaching it openly, I will not do it by taking an absurd title for my sermon; for the gospel shall stand or fall on its own merits, and with no enticing words of man's wisdom will I preach it." Let anyone say to me, "Come and give your able advocacy for this or that reform," and my answer would be, "I do not know anything about that subject, for I have determined not to know anything among you, save Jesus Christ, and Him crucified."

As Albert Barnes very well says, "This should be the resolution of every minister of the gospel. This is his business—not to be a politician; not to engage in the strifes and controversies of men; not to be merely a good farmer, or scholar; not to mingle with his people in festive circles and enjoyments; not to be a man of taste and philosophy, and distinguished mainly for refinement of manners; not to be a profound philosopher or metaphysician, but to make Christ crucified the grand object of his attention, and to seek always and everywhere to make Him known. He is not to be ashamed anywhere of the humbling doctrine that Christ was crucified. In this, he is to glory. Though the world may ridicule, though philosophers may sneer, though the rich and the socialite may deride it, yet this is to be the grand object of interest to him; and at no time, and in no society, is he to be ashamed of it. It matters not what are the amusements of society around him, what fields of science, or gain, or ambition, are open before him; the minister of Christ is to know Christ and Him crucified alone. If he cultivates science, it is to be that he may the more successfully explain and vindicate the gospel. If he becomes in any manner familiar with the works of art and of taste, it is that he may more successfully show to those who cultivate them the superior beauty and excellence of the cross. If he studies the plans and the employments of men, it is that he may more successfully meet them in those plans, and more successfully speak to them of the great plan of redemption.

"The preaching of the cross is the only kind of preaching that will be attended with success. That which has in it much respecting the Divine mission, the dignity, the works, the doctrines, the person, and the atonement of Christ, will be successful. So it was in the time of the apostles; so it was in the Reformation; so it was in the Moravian missions; so it has been in all revivals of religion. There is a power about that kind of preaching which philosophy and human reason have not. 'Christ is God's great ordinance' for the salvation of the world; and we meet the crimes and alleviate the woes of the world just in proportion as we hold the cross up as appointed to overcome the one, and to pour the balm of consolation into the other."

Would that all ministers would keep this in mind, that they should do nothing outside the office of the ministry, that to be once a minister is to be a minister forever, and never to be a politician, never to be a lecturer; that to be once a preacher is to be a preacher of Christ's holy gospel until Christ takes us to Himself to begin to sing the new song before the throne.

Now, brethren and sisters, I have discharged my duty in saying these things. If they apply to any ministers whom you admire, I cannot help it. There is the text, and what do we learn from it but this, that the apostle Paul determined to do everything as a minister of Christ? And, my dear brethren and sisters, it is your duty to do this as hearers. As Christians, it is your duty and privilege to know nothing but Jesus Christ, and Him crucified.

The Doctrines You Believe

And first, with regard to THE DOCTRINES WHICH YOU BELIEVE, I beseech you, do not know anything except Jesus Christ, and Him crucified.

You are told by one person that such-and-such a system of theology is based upon the soundest principles of reason. You are told by another that the old doctrines which you have believed are not consistent with these advanced times. You will now and then be met by smart young gentlemen who will tell you that, to be what is called a Calvinist, is to be a long way behind this progressive age; "for you know," they say, "that intellectual preachers are rising up, and that it would be well if you would become a little more intellectual in the matter of preaching and hearing."

When such a remark as that is made to any one of you, I beseech you to give this answer, "I know nothing but Jesus Christ, and Him crucified. If you can tell me more about Christ than I know, I will thank you; if you can instruct me as to how I may become more like Christ, how I may live nearer in fellowship with Him, how my faith in Him may become stronger, and my belief in His holy gospel may become more firm, then I will thank you; but if you have nothing to tell me except some intellectual lore which you have with great pains accumulated, I will tell you that, although it may be a very good thing for you to preach, and for others who are intellectual to hear, I do not belong to your class, nor do I wish to belong to it; I belong to that sect everywhere spoken against, who after the way that men call heresy worship the Lord God of their fathers, believing all things that are written in the law and in the prophets.

"I belong to a race of people who believe that it is not the pride of intellect, nor the pomp of knowledge that can teach men spiritual things. I belong to those who think that out of the mouths of babes and sucklings God has ordained strength, and I do not believe that out of your mouth God has ordained any strength at all. I belong to those who like to sit, with Mary, at the feet of Jesus, and to receive just what Christ said, as Christ said it, and because Christ said it. I want no truth but what He says is truth, and no other ground for believing it but that He says it, and no better proof that it is true than that I feel and know it to be true as applied to my own heart."

Now, dear friend, if you can do that, I will trust you anywhere—even among the wisest heretics of the age. You may go where false doctrines are rife, but you will never catch the plague of heresy while you have this golden preservative of truth, and can say, "I know nothing but Jesus Christ, and Him crucified." As for myself, I can truly say that Jesus Christ, and Him crucified is the sum of all knowledge to me; He is the highest intellectualism; He is the grandest philosophy to which my mind can attain; He is the pinnacle that rises loftier than my highest aspirations; and deeper than this great truth I wish never to fathom. Jesus Christ and Him crucified is the sum total of all I want to know, and of all the doctrines which I profess and preach.

Your Experience

Next, it must be just the same in YOUR EXPERIENCE. Brethren, I beseech you, in your experience, know nothing except Jesus Christ, and Him crucified.

You may go out tomorrow, not merely into the outside world, but into the church, the nominal church, and you will meet with a class of persons who take you by the ear, and who invite you into their houses, and the moment you are there, they begin to talk to you about the doctrines of the gospel. They say nothing about Christ Jesus; but they begin at once to talk of the eternal decrees of God, of election, and of the high mysteries of the covenant of grace. While they are talking to you, you say in your hearts, "What they are saying is true, but there is one lamentable defect in it all; their teaching is truth apart from Christ." Conscience whispers, "The election that I believe is election in Christ. These people do not talk anything about that, but only of election. The redemption that I believe always has a very special reference to the cross of Christ. They do not mention Christ; they talk of redemption as a commercial transaction, and say nothing about Jesus. With regard to final perseverance, I believe all that these men say; but I have been taught that the saints only persevere in consequence of their relation to Christ, and these men say nothing about that."

This minister, they say, is not sound, and that other minister is not sound; and let me tell you that if you get among this class of persons, you will learn to rue the day that ever you looked them in the face. If you must come into contact with them, I beseech you to say to them, "I love all the truths that you hold, but my love of them can never overpower and supersede my love to Jesus Christ, and Him crucified; and I tell you plainly, while I could not sit to hear erroneous doctrine, I could just as soon do that as sit to hear the truthful doctrine apart from the Lord Jesus Christ. I could not go to a place where I saw a man, dressed in gorgeous robes, who pretended to be Christ, and was not; and, on the other hand, I could not go to a place where I saw Christ's real robes, but the Master Himself was absent; for what I want is, not His robe, not His dress, I want the Master Himself; and if you preach to me dry doctrine without Jesus Christ, I tell you it will not suit my experience; for my experience is just this, that while I know my election, I never can know it except I know my union with the Lamb. I tell you plainly that I know I am redeemed, but I cannot bear to think of redemption without thinking of the Savior who redeemed me. It is my boast that I shall to the end endure, but I know—each hour makes me know—that my endurance depends upon my standing in Christ, and I must have that truth preached in connection with the cross of Christ."

O have nothing to do with these people, unless it is to set them right; for you will find that they are full of the gall of bitterness, the poison of asps is under their tongue. Instead of giving you things whereon your soul can feed, they will make you full of all manner of bitterness, and malice, and evil speaking against those who truly love the Lord Jesus, but who differ from them in some slight matter.

You may meet with another class of persons who will take you by the other ear, and say to you, "We, too, love Christ's doctrines, but we believe that our friends on the other side of the road are wrong. They do not preach enough experience"; and you say, "Well, I think I am not among the people who will suit me now"; and you hear the minister insisting that the most precious experience in the world is to know your own corruption, to feel the evil of the human heart, to have that filthy dunghill turned over and over in all its reeking noisomeness, and exposed before the sun; and after hearing the sermon, which is full of pretended humility, you rise from your seats more proud than you ever were in your lives, determined now that you will begin to glory in that very thing which you once counted as dross. The things which you were ashamed once to speak of, you now think should be your boast. That deep experience which was your disgrace shall now become the crown of your rejoicing. You speak to the dear brothers and sisters who imbibe this view, and they tell you to seek first, not the kingdom of God and His righteousness, but the hidden things of the prison, the discovery of the unrighteousness and unholiness of the soul.

O my dear friends, if you wish to have your lives made miserable, if you want to be led back to the bondage of Egypt, if you want to have Pharaoh's rope put round your necks once again, take their motto for your motto; but if you wish to live as I believe Christ would have you live, I would entreat you to say, "No, it does me good sometimes to hear of the evil heart, but I have made a determination to know nothing but Jesus Christ, and Him crucified, and you do not tell me anything about Him." These men preach one Sunday upon the leper; but do they preach, the next Sunday, upon the leper healed? These men tell all about the filthy state of the human heart, but they say little or nothing about that river that is to cleanse and purify it. They say much about the disease, but not so much about the Physician; and if you attend their ministry very long, you will be obliged to say, "I shall get into such a doleful condition, that I shall be tempted to imitate Judas, and go out, and hang myself. So, good morning to you, for I have determined to know nothing in my experience but Jesus Christ, and Him crucified."

I would be very earnest in trying to warn you about this matter, for there is a growing tendency, among a certain order of professing Christians, to set up something in experience except Jesus Christ, and Him crucified. Tell me that your experience is all concerned with the Lord Jesus Christ, and I will rejoice in it; the more of Christ there is in it, the more precious it is. Tell me that your experience is full of the knowledge of your own corruptions, and I answer, "If there is not in it a mixture also of the knowledge of Christ, and unless the knowledge of Christ predominates to a large degree, your experience is wood, hay, and stubble, and must be consumed, and you must suffer loss."

By the way, let me tell you a little story about Bunyan's *Pilgrim's Progress*. I am a great lover of John Bunyan, but I do not believe him infallible; and the other day I met with a story about him which I think a very good one. There was a young man in Edinburgh who wished to be a missionary. He was a wise young man; so he thought, *If I am to be a missionary, there is no need for me to transport myself far away from home; I may as well be a missionary in Edinburgh.* There's a hint to some of you ladies who give away tracts in your district and never give your servant Mary one. Well, this young man started, and determined to speak to the first person he met. He met one of these old fishwives; those of us who have seen them can never forget them, they are extraordinary women indeed. So, stepping up to her, he said, "Here you are, coming along with your burden on your back; let me ask you if you have got another burden, a spiritual burden." "What!" she asked; "do you mean that burden in John Bunyan's *Pilgrim's Progress*? Because, if you do, young man, I got rid of that many years ago, probably before you were born. But I went a better way to work than the pilgrim did. The evangelist that John Bunyan talks about was one of your parsons who do not preach the gospel; for he said, 'Keep that light in thine eye, and run to the wicket-gate.' Why, man alive! that was not the place for him to run to. He should have said, 'Do you see the cross? Run there at once!' But, instead of that, he sent the poor pilgrim to the wicket-gate first; and much good he got by going there! He got tumbling into the slough, and was like to have been killed by it."

"But did not you," the young man asked, "go through any Slough of Despond?" "Yes, I did; but I found it a great deal easier going through with my burden off than with it on my back." The old woman was quite right. John Bunyan put the getting rid of the burden too far off from the commencement of the pilgrimage. If he meant to show what usually happens, he was right; but if he meant to show what ought to have happened, he was wrong. We must not say to the sinner, "Now, sinner, if you will be saved, go to the baptismal pool; go to the wicket-gate; go to the church; do this or that." No, the cross should be right in front of the wicket-gate; and we should say to the sinner, "Throw yourself down there, and you are safe; but you are not safe till you can cast off your burden, and lie at the foot of the cross, and find peace in Jesus."

Your Faith

Let me conclude by saying, brethren and sisters, determine, from this hour, that IN YOUR FAITH you will know nothing but Jesus Christ, and Him crucified.

I am perfectly certain that I have not a grain of my own merit to trust in, and not so much as an atom of creature strength to rely upon; but I find myself often, during the seven days of the week, relying upon merit of my own that does not exist, and depending upon strength of my own which I at the same time confess has no existence at all. You and I often call the Pope antichrist; but do we not ourselves often play the antichrist, too? The Pope sets himself up as the head of the Church; but do not we go further by setting ourselves up sometimes to be our own saviors? We do not say so, except in a sort of still small voice, like the mutterings of the old wizards. It is not a loud, outspoken lie, because we should know then how to answer it; "but now," whispers the devil, "how well you did that!" and then we begin to rely upon our works, and Satan says, "You prayed so well yesterday, you will never be cold in your prayers again; and you will be so strong in faith that you will never doubt your God again."

It is the old golden calf that is set up once more; for, although it was ground to powder, it seems to have the art of coming together again. After we have been told, ten times over, that we cannot have any merit of our own, we begin to act as if we had; and the man who tells you, in his doctrine, that all his fresh springs are in Christ, yet thinks and acts just as if he had fresh springs of his own. He mourns as if all his dependence were upon himself, and groans as if his salvation depended upon his own merits. We often get talking, in our own souls, as if we did not believe the gospel at all, but were hoping to be saved by our own works, and our own creature performances.

O for a stronger determination to know nothing henceforth but Jesus Christ, and Him crucified! I would to God that I could make that resolution myself, and that you would all make it with me. I heard once of a countryman who was preaching one day, and he preached very nicely the first half of his sermon. But, toward the end he entirely broke down, and his brother said to him, "Tom, I can tell you why you did not preach well at the end of your sermon. It was because you got on so nicely at the first that the devil whispered, 'Well done, Tom, you are getting on very well'; and as soon as the devil said that, you thought 'Tom is a very fine fellow,' and then the Lord left you." Happy would it have been for Tom if he could have determined to know nothing but Jesus Christ, and Him crucified, and not to have known Tom at all. That is what I desire to know myself; for I know nothing but the power which comes from on high, I never can be less powerful at one time than at another, and I can glory in my infirmity because it makes room for Christ's power to rest upon me.

> I glory in infirmity,
> That Christ's own power may rest on me:
> When I am weak, then am I strong,
> Grace is my shield, and Christ my song.

It should be a good resolution for you, brethren, and for myself, to determine to know nothing about ourselves, and nothing about our own doings. Now, friend John, begin to think nothing about yourself, and to know nothing but Jesus Christ. Let John go where he likes, and be you relying not upon John's strength, but upon Christ's. And you, Peter, know nothing about Peter at all, and do not boast, "Though all men should deny you, yet will I never deny you"; but know that Peter's Lord Jesus is living inside Peter, and then you may go on comfortably enough.

Determine, Christian, that, by the grace of God, it shall be your endeavor to keep your eye single, to keep your faith fixed alone on the Lord Jesus; without any addition of your own works, or your own strength; and determining that, you may go on your way rejoicing, singing of the cross of Christ as your boast, your glory, and your all. We are now coming to the table of our Master, and I hope that this will be our determination there, to know nothing save Jesus Christ, and Him crucified; and may the Lord give us His blessing! Amen.

7
Christ Set Forth as a Propitiation[*]

Christ Jesus whom God hath set forth to be a propitiation through faith in his blood (Romans 3:25).

We commenced the services in this place by the declaration that here Christ shall be preached; our brother who followed us expressed his joy that Christ was preached, herein he did rejoice, yea, and would rejoice; and our friends must have observed, how, throughout the other services there has been a most blessed admixture not only of the true spirit of Christ, but of pointed and admirable reference to the glories and beauties of His person. This morning, which is the beginning of our more regular and constant ministry, we come again to the same noble theme. Christ Jesus is today to be set forth. You will not charge me as repeating myself—you will not look up to the pulpit and say, "Pulpits are places of tautology"; you will not reply that you have heard this story so often that you have grown weary with it, for well I know that with you the person, the character, and the work of Christ are always fresh themes for wonder.

We have seen the sea, some of us hundreds of times, and what an abiding sameness there is in its deep green surface, but who ever called the sea monotonous? Traveling over it as the mariner does, sometimes by the year together, there is always a freshness in the undulation of the waves, the whiteness of the foam of the breaker, the curl of the crested billow, and the frolicsome pursuit of every wave by its long train of brothers.

Which of us has ever complained that the sun gave us but little variety—that at morn he yoked the same steeds, and flashed from his car the same golden glory, climbed with dull uniformity the summit of the skies, then drove his chariot downward, and bade his flaming coursers steep their burning fetlocks in the western deep?

---

* This sermon was preached on Good Friday morning, March 29, 1861, at the Metropolitan Tabernacle, Newington, and is taken from *The Metropolitan Tabernacle Pulpit.*

82

Who among us has complained of the monotony of the bread that we eat? We eat it today, tomorrow, the next day; we have eaten it for years that are passed, and though we have other savory matters therewith, yet still the one unvarying food is served upon the table, and the bread remains the staff of life.

Surely I know that as Christ is your food and your spiritual bread; as Christ is your sun, your heavenly light; as Christ is the sea of love in which your passions swim, and all your joys are found, it is not possible that you as Christians should complain of a monotony in Him, "He is the same yesterday, today, and forever"; and yet He has the dew of His youth. He is the manna in the golden pot which was always the same, but He is the manna which came from heaven which was every morning new. He is the rod of Moses which was dry, and changed not its shape, but He is also to us the rod of Aaron which buds and blossoms and brings forth almonds.

I come then now to preach Christ crucified, as God has set Him forth to be a propitiation for us through faith in His blood. To begin at once then we shall notice first, *what is meant here by God's setting forth Christ as a propitiation*; secondly, we shall dwell upon the truth which may very naturally be drawn from the first—*Christ the propitiation, as looked upon by the believer*; and then, thirdly, putting the two together, I mean inverting the two thoughts, we shall look at *Christ as set forth by us, and looked upon by God.*

A Propitiation

First then, the text says of Christ Jesus, "WHOM GOD HATH SET FORTH TO BE A PROPITIATION THROUGH FAITH IN HIS BLOOD."

The words "set forth" in the original may signify "fore-ordained"; but according to eminent critics it has also in it the idea of our translation of setting forth as well as a "fore-ordinance." Barnes says, "The word properly means *to place in public view*; to exhibit in a conspicuous situation, as goods are exhibited or exposed for sale, or as premiums or rewards of victory were exhibited to public view in the games of the Greeks." So has God the Father set forth, manifested, made conspicuous the person of the Lord Jesus as the propitiation of sin. How has He done this? He has done it first by *ordaining Him in the divine decree* as the propitiation of sin. Christ did not take upon Himself the office of High Priest without being chosen thereunto as was Aaron. As surely as every member of Christ's body is elect according to the foreknowledge of God, as certainly as in God's book all His members were written which in continuance were fashioned when as yet there was none of them, so certainly was the Head Himself ordained the chosen of God. As our poet puts it—

Christ be my first elect he said,
Then chose our souls in Christ our Head.

Perhaps some might say there could be no election where there was no
room for choice. But how do we know that there was no room for choice?
We can scarce imagine that angel or archangel could have been set forth
as propitiation for sin; yet who can tell whether the Almighty mind might
not have devised another plan? Who shall dare to limit the Holy One of
Israel? At any rate, there was this choice between the Father, the Son, and
the Holy Spirit: the Divine wisdom, conjoined with Divine Sovereignty,
chose, and appointed, and determined that Christ Jesus, the second of the
Mysterious Three, should be the propitiation for our sins. When Christ
came into the world, He came as one of whom all eternity had spoken; He
is the child born—born from the womb of destiny; He is the Lamb whom
God had appointed from before the foundation of the world. Long before
this world was made, or Adam fell, Christ had been set forth. In the volume of the Book it had been written of Him, "I delight to do thy will, O
God."

I think those who are afraid of looking back upon the great decrees of
God because they say they are secrets, have a fear where no fear is. There
is never fear, my brethren, of our meddling with secret things; if they be
secret, it is quite certain that we shall not meddle with them. Only let it be
announced once for all that they are secret; and there is no one who *can*
betray the secrets of God. But things that are revealed belong to us and to
our children; and this is one of the things that is revealed, this is the decree,
and we will declare it, the Lord said unto Christ, "Thou art my Son; this
day have I begotten thee"; and He has said unto Him moreover, "I will
make him my first-born, higher than the kings of the earth." And all this,
that He may be the "propitiation for our sins by faith in His blood."

And next, God had set forth Christ to be a propitiation for sins *in His
promises before the advent.* Did He not set Him forth most plainly in the
garden where we fell? Was He not plainly revealed afterward in the ark in
which Noah was saved? Did not God speak constantly, not only by verbal
promises, but by typical promises, which are just as sure and certain as
those which are spoken in words? Did He not to a hundred seers, and to
multitudes of holy men and women, constantly reveal the coming of Him
who should bruise the serpent's head, and deliver His people from the
power of the curse?

It is wonderful to see how engaged the Holy Spirit was through every
age and era in ordaining types, in bringing forth representations and sym-
bols in which Christ should be set forth as being the appointed propitiation
for sins through faith in His blood. But the great setting forth was *the actual doing of the deed* when Jesus Christ came forth from the chambers of

mystery and revealed Himself in the manger—when God set Him forth by angelic messengers appointed to be His attendants, set Him forth by the star in the East which should guide the distant strangers to the place where the young child was. When He set Him forth afterward by preserving His life in the midst of imminent perils, fulfilling promises made concerning His infancy in the place where He was hidden from Herod's fury, and in the spot where He was educated and brought up.

Throughout the life of Christ, how constantly did His Father set Him forth! The voice of God was in the voice of John—"Behold the Lamb of God which taketh away the sins of the world." And on the cross itself, "when it pleased the Father to bruise him, and put him to grief," what an exhibition was there of Christ to the eye of Jew and Gentile, of prince and peasant, of the learned Greek, of the ruder Roman—that God had appointed Christ to be the full propitiation for sin. I think, my dear friends, while we must always regard the cross as being the representation of Christ's love to His Church, we must also view it as being God setting forth to man the way by which He will accept man, pardon his sin, hear his prayer, and be reconciled with His erring creatures.

But, O my dear friends, this is not all; God the Father set forth Christ since then by signs following. What a setting forth that was of Christ the propitiator, *when the Holy Spirit came down* on Pentecost! And what have all conversions been since then? Have they not been repeated seals to the testimony that Christ is the appointed Redeemer of men, and that through Him the faithful are justified and accepted? You, I trust, have many of you had such a special setting forth of Christ in your own hearts, that you can set your seal to the text before us for Him has God set forth in you as being the propitiation. By effectual grace your eyes have been opened; by infinite love your stubborn heart has been melted; you have been turned from every other hope and every other refuge; you have seen Christ to be the power of God and the wisdom of God; constrained by an omnipotent influence which you neither could nor would resist, you have received Him as the sent of God, have taken Him as being God's Messiah and your only refuge. God *in you*, then, has graciously fulfilled the text, "Him hath God set forth to be a propitiation."

But now, to change the subject for a moment, and yet to continue on the same point, *what is it that God has so manifestly set forth*? We have seen *how* He has done it—we turn now to *what*? Sinner, listen, and if you have already accepted that which the Father has revealed, let your joy become full. God has set forth Christ as being a propitiation. The original Greek word has the meaning: a mercy seat or a covering. Now God has said to the sinner, "Do you desire to meet Me? Would you be no longer My enemy? Could you tell Me your sorrows? Would you receive My blessing? Would you establish a commerce between your

Creator and your soul? I set forth Christ to you as being the mercy seat, where I can meet with you and you can meet with Me." Or take the word as signifying a covering; as the mercy seat covered the tables of the law, and so covered that which was the cause of Divine ire, because we had broken His commandment.

"Would you have anything which can cover your sin? Cover it from Me, your God, so that I need not be provoked to anger; cover it from Me so that you need not be cowed with excessive fear, and tremble to approach Me as you did when I came in thunders and lightnings upon Sinai? Would you have a shelter which shall hide altogether your sins and iniquities? I set it forth to you in the person of My bleeding Son. Trust in His blood, and your sin is covered from My eyes; nay, it shall be covered from your own eyes too; and being justified by faith, you have grace to accept now what God the Father sets forth!" The Romish priest sets forth this and that; our own Romish hearts set forth such-and-such-another thing; but God sets forth *Christ*. The preacher of doctrine sets forth a *dogma*; the preacher of experience sets forth a *feeling*; the preacher of practice often sets forth an *effort*; but God puts before you *Christ*. "Here will I meet with you." This is the place of My rest—glorious to Me, safe to you. Come to Christ! "Come to Christ, and you will come to Me." The Lord Almighty comes to Christ, and there He comes to you. God, then, has set forth Christ Jesus; made Him conspicuous as being the mercy-seat and the great hider of sin.

What has He set forth? He has set forth Christ before every one of you, in the daily preaching of the Word, and in the Inspired Book, as His anointed to do His work, suffering in the stead and place of all who believe on Him. He has set Him forth as nailed to Calvary's cross, that your sins might be nailed there. Set Him forth as dying, that your sins might die; nay, buried that your iniquities might be buried; risen, that you might rise to newness of life; ascended, that you might ascend to God; received in triumph, that you might be received in triumph too; made to reign, that you might reign in Him, forever loved, forever crowned, that you in Him may be forever loved and forever crowned too. Him has God the Father set forth, that by faith in His blood your sins being put away, you might enjoy the blessing of complete justification. "Who is He that condemneth? Christ hath died, yea rather, hath risen again, and sitteth at the right hand of God, who also maketh intercession for us." "Who shall say anything to the charge of God's elect?" Thus, then, and in these respects, has God the Father set forth Christ.

The Believer and That Propitiation

And now I proceed in the second place—and may the Spirit of God descend more visibly into our midst than at present—to speak upon a duty, a privilege rather, which so naturally rises out of God's having shown forth His Son as being the propitiation through faith in His blood. That privilege is that WE SHOULD LOOK TO CHRIST, AND LOOK TO CHRIST ALONE AS THE PROPITIATION FOR OUR SINS, AND TAKE CARE THAT OUR FAITH BE SIMPLE, AND FIXED SOLELY ON HIS PRECIOUS BLOOD.

A very common mistake is to look to our sense of need as being at least in some degree a propitiation for sin. Repentance is an absolute duty, and a Christian grace—a grace without which there can be no salvation. But there has been a strong temptation upon many minds to make repentance a preparation for Christ, and to regard a sense of need as being a kind of wedding garment in which they may approach the Savior. How many read that promise, "Come unto me all ye that are weary and heavy laden, and I will give you rest," and they fondly imagine that if they could be more weary and more heavily laden then they would have rest? Whereas, being weary and heavy laden gives no man rest. It is coming to Christ that gives him rest; it is not the being weary and the being heavy laden.

And I have known some ministers who preach what is called a deep experience and law work, and preach very rightly too, because many of the people of God have to endure this; but I think they lead the people into error, for the people imagine that this law work, this deep experience has something to do with the propitiation of their sins. Now, my hearers, the sins of God's people are taken already by the blood of Christ, and not by any repentance of their own. I have already guarded my statement, and now I will make it as bold as possible. I say that repentance of sin in no wise contributes to the removal of that sin meritoriously. I say that our sense of need does not take away our guilt, nor help to take it away; but the blood, the blood, the blood alone, pure and unmixed, has forever washed the people of God, and made them whiter than snow.

So, poor heart, if your soul be as hard as a nether millstone, if your conscience seems to be seared by long habits of sin, if you cannot force tears from your eyes, and scarce can get a groan from your heart, yet you are groaning today because you cannot groan, weeping because you cannot weep, and sorrowing because you cannot sorrow. Hear, then, this gospel message, God the Father has set Christ forth to be your propitiation; not your tender conscience, not your groans, not your sense of need, not your law work, not your deep experience. He is enough without any of these; have faith in His blood and you are saved.

But again, many have fallen into another mistake. They make their propitiation depend upon their evidences. I would be the last to say, "Away with evidences, away with evidences," for they are good things in their proper place; but there are so many persons who always judge of their past conversion and ultimate salvation by present evidence. Judge, brethren, whether you could ever form a proper estimate of the world by its appearance on any one day. If I had taken you out a month ago into the fields, you would have declared that the trees were dead. What signs of life would you have perceived? The bulbs were buried in the ground; you might have taken a solemn oath that flowers were banished, and you might have imagined that because there were none, there never would be any.

But what was your evidence of the world's state worth? Look at it now, when the buds are bursting on the trees, when the flowers are springing from the sod, when everything is hastening on toward spring and summer. Why, as it is absurd and ridiculous for us to judge of the world's estate by the fact that there was a cloud today and there was a shower of rain yesterday, and therefore infer that the sun has lost its force and will never shine; it is just as ridiculous to judge of our standing before God by our present standing, according to our evidences on some one day.

The right way to read evidences is this. First, my soul, whether you are saved or not, look to Christ as a poor guilty sinner. When you have done this, then read your evidences; then, *not till then*. Then the blessed evidence will be a confirmation; the witness of the Spirit will confirm your faith. But if you look to your evidences first you will be foolish indeed. It is as in a reflector; first, let us have the light, then will the reflector be of use to us to increase and reflect back the light; but if I take my reflector into a dark place, and look for light in it, I shall find none. I must first see to the light itself, and then to the reflection of it.

Our graces are the reflection of Christ's love; they are the tokens of it, but we had better go to Christ first, and then look to the tokens afterward. I am sure if you, as a spouse, had offended your husband, you would find but very sorry comfort in looking at those little tokens of love which in the past he had conferred on you. You would go to him first, ask him whether his love was still firm, whether he had forgiven the fault, and when you had received the assurance of his unabated and pure affection, then could you go upstairs to the secret drawer and look over the love notes and the love tokens, but they would have afforded you sorry comfort before.

So with any child who has been chastened by his parent, if he thinks that his father is angry with him, he will not, if he be a wise child, a simple-hearted child, go up to the nursery and look at the gifts which his father gave him, but going to his father's knee he will look up, with a tear in his eye, and say, "Father do you love me; can you forgive your child?" And, when he has had the personal token, the kiss of acceptance, then may the child go back and see in every mouthful that he eats, and every garment which he wears, the sure token of his father's continued affection. Evidences are good as second things, but as first things they are usurpers, and may prove anti-Christs to Christ. Whatever my evidences may say, if I believe in the precious blood, there is not a sin against me in God's book, and in the teeth of everything which might make me tremble.

> Just as I am, without one plea,
> But that His blood was shed for me
> And that He bids me come.

I come again, and come afresh to him whom God has set forth to be the propitiation for our sins.

Friends, I may surprise you by what I am about to say, but there is another fault into which we sometimes fall, namely, looking to God's promises instead of looking to Christ as the propitiation of sin. The text does not say that God the Father has set forth promises. Indeed He has given us exceeding great and precious promises, and they are true *in Christ.* We often err by going to promises instead of going to Christ. I know many Christians who, when they are in distress, take up the Bible to find a promise—a very good and a very admirable plan, if, mark, it be preceded by something else. If they go to Christ first, they may come to the promise afterward. "Yes," says one, "but suppose a promise be applied." Very good; you have comfort out of it, but I say suppose the promise is not applied, what then? Why, it is just as sure for all that; whether the promise is applied or not. Application is not my duty; my business is to take Christ whom God the Father has set forth as the propitiation of my sins, and if in searching this book through, there is not a single promise which I dare lay hold of, if I cannot find one bottle filled with the rich wine of consolation; if I can lay hold on no bunch of the grapes of Eshcol, still God the Father has set forth *Christ* whatever else He has not set forth, and my eye looks to Christ and to Christ alone.

There is a man who very much desires an estate, at the same time his heart is smitten with the beauty of some fair heiress. He gets the title-deeds of her estate. Well, the title-deeds are good, but the estates are not his, though he has the title-deeds. By-and-by he marries the lady, and everything is his own. Get the heiress and you have the estate. It is so in Christ: promises are the title-deeds of His estates. A man may get the promise and not get Christ, and then they will be of no more use to him than the deeds of another man's estate would be to me, if I be not the lawful proprietor; but when my soul is married unto Christ, then I am heir of all things in Him and with Him.

Why, Christian, what right have you to say "that promise is not mine because it is not applied"? Your right to the promise does not lie in its being applied, nor yet in our power to lay hold of it. Every promise that is in the Bible belongs to every man who is in Christ, and belongs to him as much one day as another day, because Christ is his at all times, evermore the same. Oh! I do not know whether I can put this exactly as I mean it, but

I mean this, that the devil has often tempted me with, "You have not had a promise sent home to your heart for months, you are no child of God, you cannot get that sweetness out of such-and-such a passage that some men can." I reply to Satan in this way: "Well, God has never said He has set forth the promise to be a propitiation through faith but He *has* set forth Christ, and my soul accepts that which God has set forth, and if never promise be applied to me, the promise is mine for all that, and in faith I will lay hold on it and defy thee to rob me of it when my soul has laid hold on Christ." O that we lived more on Christ and less on anything but Christ, nearer to Christ's person, more surely resting on Christ's blood, more simply accepting Him as our all in all.

I have not yet done on this second head. A remark or two suggest themselves to me now. God has set forth Christ to be the propitiation through faith in His blood, and we ought to accept Christ as being an *all-sufficient* propitiation. I believe in Christ today; but if some sin lies upon my conscience, and I am worried and troubled about it, ought I not to perceive at once that I have failed to accept Christ as an all-sufficient propitiation? Whether my sin be little or be great, whether it be fresh or old, it is the same sin, and, blessed be God, has all been atoned for through Christ the propitiation. We ought to take Christ as being the death of every sin and of all sin, as having expunged and wiped out the great debt as well as the little; the ten thousand talents as well as the one hundred pence. We will never have the full idea of Christ till we know that every sin of thought, of word, of deed that the believer has ever been guilty of, finds its death, its total annihilation in the propitiation which God has set forth. Oh! we want to come where Kent was, when he said—

> Now free from sin I walk at large,
> My Savior's blood's my full discharge,
> At His dear feet my soul I lay,
> A sinner saved and homage pay.

Well, but when we have come as far as this, we need to add a second thought. God has set forth Christ to be not only an all-sufficient but an *immutable* propitiation for sin. Christ is as much my soul's propitiation, when my soul has fallen into sin, as when I have stood firm and resisted temptation, if I be a believer. "That is putting it," you say, "in a bold and almost Antinomian way." I cannot help it; it is true—it is true that the propitiation of Christ is never more, never less. It cannot be more, it is complete; it cannot be less, for it is the same yesterday, today, and forever. That man who has been washed in blood is white; his doubts and fears have not spoiled that whiteness; his powerlessness yesterday in prayer, his despondency a week ago, his all but complete unbelief last month, do not mar the perfection of Jesus' righteousness—do not take away from the complete achievement of the pardon of his sin by precious blood. I do believe, and hold, and rejoice in that precious truth, that our standing before God, when we have believed in Jesus, depends no more upon our frames and our feelings, than the sun itself in its native glory depends upon the clouds and darkness that are here below. The same—the same in all its splendor, the same undimmed, as full of glory, as full of majesty, the right-eousness and blood of Christ abides; and we, standing before God in Him, and not in ourselves, are ever complete in Him—ever accepted in the beloved: never more so, never less so. "Strong meat this," says one. Be it strong: nothing short of this will ever satisfy the tried Christian in the hour when sin rolls over his head. If any man can make a bad use of the doctrine of the real substitution of Christ, and the standing of Christ's people in Christ's place every day—if any man can make a licentious use of that, his damnation is just; he has no part nor lot in this matter. But I know this, that I am not to be restrained from the comfort of a doctrine because some licentious vagabond chooses to destroy his soul with it. Still there stands the glorious truth; and nothing short of this is the full glory of Christ's atonement: that when once He shed His blood, and when once that blood has been applied to us, by it and it alone we stand completely pure, and are as pure one day as another day; perfect, complete, accepted, made secure and safe in Christ Jesus the Lord. "Him hath God the Father set forth to be a propitiation for sin." My soul accepts Him today as it did yes-terday, and knows that the sin is put away forever.

Christ, as God Looks at Him

Now I shall come to my third and last point. Turn the thoughts over. We have said God sets forth Christ, and we look at it. Now, as a matter of duty and privilege, we must SET FORTH CHRIST, AND GOD WILL LOOK AT HIM.

The preacher, standing here as he does today before this immense assembly, knows that without God's looking upon the ministry it will be vain and void. How shall God's eye be secured?—how shall His presence be guaranteed? If in this pulpit Christ be set forth, God will look down upon that Christ set forth, and honor and bless the Word. Brethren, I might preach clear doctrine, but God might never look down upon doctrine; for I could point you to churches with a tear in my eye, because I am able to do so, where conversions are rare things. The doctrine is high, high enough; perhaps so high as to have become putrid. I will not say that, but I do know some churches where there has not been an addition to the church by the stretch of ten or a dozen years together, and I have known the reason. Christ was not set forth, and therefore God did not look down on what was set forth, because it was the wrong thing. I have known, too, churches—and with equal sorrow do I mention them—where practice has been preached, but not Christ. People have been exhorted to do ten thousand things; moral duties presented before the people in pleasing and well-polished essays have taken the place of the cross of Christ, and there have been no conversions; by degrees the attendance has become very slender; for where Christ is not preached, it is a strange thing there are some exceptions to the rule, but still the rule is—there are not many to listen. Only preach Socinianism, and what a splendid hunting-ground this tabernacle will be for the spiders! Give up Christ and preach philosophy, you need not have an organ and a skillful person to play the people out of the church: they would never need that; they will never come in.

So is it. Those flimsy doctrines never can prevail, because no one will listen to them; they are not attractive; they look as if they would attract all; but none can receive them. The secret being that God will not look down on any man's ministry unless that man sets forth what God sets forth, even Christ Jesus as the propitiation for sin. It is not a question as to whether there will be conversions when Christ is set forth; that is certain. Some good brethren quote the text, "Paul *may* plant, and Apollos *may* water, *but*"—and they are a long while upon the "but," and they pervert the text a little, "but God gives the increase." Now the text does not say any such thing. It says, "Paul planteth and Apollos watereth, God giveth the increase." They are all linked together; Paul does not plant in vain, Apollos does not water in vain; God gives the increase—sure to do it, and if there be not souls saved, there is always some reason for it; and the reason to which I would look—leaving now the inscrutable sovereignty of God out of the question for a moment—the reason would be either that Christ is not preached, or else He is preached in such a way as He never ought to be preached—with cold-heartedness, with want of zeal, with lack of tenderness.

Only let Christ be preached by an earnest heart, though there be no eloquence, though the elocution be defective, Christ being set forth, God the Holy Spirit will come forth too, and the Word must and will be blessed. His Word shall not return unto Him void; it shall prosper in the thing whereto He has sent it.

But again, as in the ministry we must set forth Christ if we would have God's smile, so you my brothers and sisters in your pleadings for the souls of men must set forth Christ. What a mass of wickedness is hereabouts; what tens of thousands in this immediate neighborhood who know nothing of God. Here is a city with very nearly three million inhabitants; it is not a city but an empire in itself. What shall we do when we are on our knees? I confess I have sometimes found myself utterly unable to express my desires in prayer to God for this city. When you once get a notion of its sin, its infamy, its dens, its innumerable missionaries teaching Satanic doctrines, its multitudes of men and women whose livelihood it is to ensnare the simple ones, it is an awful burden to carry before God, you cannot pray for London except in sighs and groans.

Good old Roby Flockhart, who stood for many years in the streets of Edinburgh, and used to be much laughed at, but who preached every night in the week, and had during the winter months a little lantern which he put upon a stick and then stood in a corner and preached to the passers by, with a great power, but much eccentricity. That good man was eminent in his prayers when alone. A gentleman told me that he went one night to see poor Robert, he was extremely poor; the candle had been blown out and he stumbled his way up two or three pair of stairs and came at last to Flockhart's room; he opened the door and he could not see the good old man, but he could hear him say, "O Lord, dinna forget Edinboro', dinna forget Edinboro', turn not away thine hand from auld Reeki, dinna forget her. Lord; thy servant will never give thee rest till thou pour out thy spirit upon Edinboro'."

My friend stood still, and there was that old man alone with his God; my friend had never heard such groaning and crying; it seemed as if he could even hear the falling of his tears while he prayed for God to bless Edinburgh, and to pour out His spirit upon that city. He made some noise, and the old man said, "There is somebody there I suppose." He struck a light and found he had taken one of the pillows of his bed to kneel upon by the side of an old chair which was about the only furniture, with the exception of the bed. He would pray for Edinburgh by the hour together, and then go out to preach, though many laughed at and hooted him.

O, one wants to feel like that for London too, kneeling there till one's knees are sore, crying, "Do not forget London, do not forget London. Lord, turn not thy face from London, but make bare thine arm in this great city." But how are we to make our prayers prevail with God? Brethren, we must show forth Christ in prayer, and then God will look upon our prayers. The Methodist cry which was once heard at the prayer-meeting when a poor Methodist brother could not go on, and someone at the far end of the chapel cried out, "Plead *the blood*, brother, plead *the blood*"—that old Methodist cry has force and power in it. "Plead the blood." God cannot, cannot, cannot, resist the cry of the blood of Christ. Abel's blood demanded vengeance, and it had it; Christ's blood demands pardons and shall have it, must have it; our God cannot be deaf to the cry of His own Son's blood; and if you and I and all of us together can plead the precious blood of Christ for London, a revival must come, will come, shall come, and the face of the times shall be changed. God's arm shall be revealed, and "all flesh shall see it together, for the mouth of the Lord hath spoken it."

Yet once again, and here with affectionate earnestness, I come to plead personally with each of you. Soul, are you this morning sick of self and longing to be saved? Do your sins condemn you; do your lusts accuse you;

does your conscience flog you? Have you been to God in prayer; have you sought for mercy; has no mercy come? Have you read the Bible to find a promise, has no promise dropped with honey to you? Come I pray you and obey the Word of God which I utter in your hearing; come and take Christ and show Christ's blood to God, and He will, He must smile upon you. If you cannot take the promise, take the blood; if you cannot come before God with any feelings come with Christ in your hands. "May I trust Christ?" asks one. *May* you! you are *commanded* to do it. He who believes not has made God a liar *because* he believes not. He who believes has set to his seal that God is true. Sinner, God is satisfied with Christ. Does He satisfy God and will He not satisfy you? The eternal Judge has accepted Jesus, and do you refuse Him? The Lord has opened the door and stands at it; is the door good enough for the king, and yet not good enough for a rebel like yourself?

"But" Away with your *"buts."* You want to bring something to add to Christ; is He enough to reconcile God, and not enough to reconcile you? "But," "but," again. So God thinks the precious blood to be a sufficient price, and you think it is not? O fool, and slow of heart, how dare you to think that God has not set forth enough but you must add to it? Instead of this, I pray you in Christ's stead, believe in Christ, as you are. Whoever you may be, whatever your past life has been, whatever your present feelings now are, entrust your soul with Christ, and God declares that your sins are put away. Put your soul as it is, I care not how black, it matters not how depraved it *is*, put it here on that mercy seat which God has set forth, and you have put it where God bade you put it, and its salvation rests no more with you, nor is it any more a matter of hazard; you have put your salvation into Christ's hands, it is His business to save you and He will do it.

> I know that safe with Him remains
> Protected by His power,
> What I've committed to His hands
> Till the decisive hour.

I do not know how it is, but this simple doctrine is the hardest doctrine to make plain. It seems so easy, and yet many *will* mystify and doubt. "What, no good works, no good feelings!" All these things are fruits of grace; but salvation does not depend upon them. Salvation is *in Christ*, wholly in Christ, in Christ alone, and the moment any of you do trust Him unfeignedly to be your sole and only Savior you have accepted God's propitiation, and God has accepted you. It is not possible for the Lord, unless He could reverse His nature, stain His honor, belie His character, make His Word a farce, and the atonement of Christ a falsehood, to reject any man under heaven who believes in Christ, and takes Him to be His all in all.

This day is called Good Friday; may it be a good Friday to some of you.

Perhaps I have some here to whom I have preached these last seven years, and yet you have remained unsaved. I am clear of your blood if you had only heard but this one morning sermon, for God witnesses I know not how to put the plan of salvation more plainly than I have done. "God has set forth Christ to be a propitiation through His blood." I bid you look to Christ bleeding, to Christ sweating drops of blood, Christ scourged, Christ nailed to the tree, and if you believe in Christ's blood, He is the propitiation of your sins.

But I can do no more than this; it is mine to preach, it is mine to pray, and mine to plead. O may God the Holy Spirit give you grace to receive, to accept, to yield to this blessed proclamation of free mercy. Other salvation there is none; you may rack your soul with pain, and wear out your bones with toil, but there is rest nowhere but here, "Believe on the Lord Jesus Christ, and thou shalt be saved." "He that with his heart believeth and is baptized shall be saved, but he that believeth not shall be damned."

What shall I say? Instead of pleading further with you I would plead with God in private, that many of you may now try whether Christ cannot save you. Rest yourself on Him, trust yourself with Him, and He will be as good as His Word, and save you now, and save you even to the end. The Lord add His blessing, for Jesus' sake. Amen.

8

The Bitterness of the Cross[*]

They. . . . shall be in bitterness for him (Zechariah 12:10).

Y ou know, dear friends, that this text primarily refers to the Jewish nation. They will not always be blinded, as they are at present. The veil will ultimately be taken away from their eyes and their heart; and when it is taken away, it will not be by the enlightenment of mere reason, or through the cogency of argument by itself, but it will be through the outpouring of the Spirit of our God. The verse from which our text is taken makes this quite clear: "I will pour upon the house of David, and upon the inhabitants of Jerusalem, the spirit of grace and of supplications."

Our Lord Jesus Christ can only be seen in His own light. The grace of God must be given to us before we can see and understand Christ at all; and this shall be the great proof that grace has been given to Israel—that they shall look upon Christ. It is good evidence that grace has been given to any man when he looks upon Christ, obeying the great command: "Look unto me, and be ye saved, all the ends of the earth." This is the first sign and token of believers, and it is to be our continual distinguishing mark, for we are always to be "looking unto Jesus, the Author and Finisher of our faith."

There is much more in a look at Christ than many suppose; it is the index of everything that appertains to the Christian life. There must be life in an eye that can see; and when there is life in the eye, there is life in the whole man who possesses that eye. When an eye can see Christ, it can see other things that he intends it to see. That eye which has been enabled to behold Him, and which has taught the heart to cry, "My Lord and my God," is prepared to see all the wondrous things that are in God's law.

The first mark of grace, then, in the Jew, will be that he shall look to Christ. By that word "look," I do not understand a mere transient glance

---

[*]   This sermon was intended for reading on Sunday, July 15, 1900, and was preached at the Metropolitan Tabernacle, Newington, on Thursday evening, May 12, 1881. It is taken from *The Metropolitan Tabernacle Pulpit.*

at Him, but a long, lingering, wistful, discerning, penetrating, loving look at Him, and unto Him, as it is in that verse, "They looked unto him, and were lightened." At first, it may be only a furtive stolen glance; but when men come to see and feel the full power of Christ, they will want to have a long, fixed, steady gaze at Him. Blessed will be the day when the Jews shall be brought even to think seriously about Christ.

At present, they will scarcely listen to the arguments concerning Him; they denounce the Nazarene, and stop their ears against His gospel; but the day shall come when they will hear, when they will hearken diligently, and incline their ear, and come unto Him that their soul may live. They shall look, and look, and look, and look, and look, until the vision shall at last break in upon their very soul, and then they shall say, "It is He! Yes, it is He of whom Moses in the law and the prophets did write. This is no other than the promised Messiah, the Son of David; and, alas! hitherto, both we and our fathers have rejected Him." And as they thus look, and realize the greatness of their guilt, they will begin to weep and lament that they have so long refused their only Savior.

So, the first effect upon the Jews of a true sight of Christ—and, as we are all constituted so much alike, the first effect upon any man who has a true sight of Christ—is that it produces sincere sorrow: "They shall look upon me whom they have pierced, and they shall mourn for him, as one mourneth for his only son, and shall be in bitterness for him, as one that is in bitterness for his firstborn." I must confess that I have no love for a dry-eyed faith. The faith that never wept over sin will have to be wept over one of these days. If you say that you have seen Christ, and yet you have never mourned over your transgressions, I think you must have seen a false christ, and not the true Son of God; for they who behold His wounds are themselves wounded, they who gaze upon His pierced heart are themselves pierced to the heart—nay, they are pierced in the heart, and they who, by faith, see the flowing of His precious blood feel their very hearts bleed on account of Him, and all that He endured on their behalf.

A sight of His crucifixion crucifies sin. A sight of His death—if it be a true sight—is the death of all love of sin. If, then, you have never felt the mournful effect of the sorrowful spectacle of the bleeding Savior, you have need still to stand, and to look, and look, and look again until you do feel it, for so it will always be: "They shall look upon me whom they have pierced, and they shall mourn."

That is the general thought of this verse: the Jews will look to Christ, and they will mourn; and the same thing happens with Gentiles, they also look to Christ, and they mourn. So the theme we are to consider is the wonderful truth that, when we rightly look to Christ, whether we are Jews or Gentiles, we are "in bitterness for him, as one that is in bitterness for his firstborn." It is quite true that, of all sights in the world, the sight of Christ crucified is the sweetest. People say, "See Naples, and die"; but it would be worth while to see Christ by faith, even if that sight were necessarily followed by death. Of all that can be seen in the world, there is nothing so delightful as a believing sight of Jesus Christ. I appeal to all of you whose eyes have ever been ravished with that wondrous vision; do you not say to your Lord—

> A glimpse—a single glimpse of Thee,
> Would more delight my soul
> Than this vain world, with all its joys,
> Could I possess the whole?

At first sight, it seems strange that the mourner turns his eyes sooner to the place called Calvary than to the sacred spot where the star of Bethlehem shone; and stranger still that there should be more delight to be found in Gabbatha and Golgotha than even in the Mount of Transfiguration. The cross of Christ is the first resort of sorrow for sin, and it is the last abode of holy grief, where she lays aside her weeds, and puts on her beautiful array. Yet there must be some bitterness always associated with Calvary; do not be startled at that thought. The command concerning the paschal lamb was, "With bitter herbs shall ye eat it"; marvel not that the Lamb of God, however sweet He is, and however nourishing to our souls, can never be enjoyed by us without the bitter herbs of godly sorrow for sin: "They shall mourn for him, as one mourneth for his only son, and shall be in bitterness for him"; and that bitterness shall be of the most intense kind: "as one that is in bitterness for his firstborn."

Our line of thought will be this. First, I want to point out to you that *our first sight of Christ brings bitterness*; then secondly, I will try to show you that *our continued sight of Christ works in us throughout life a measure of the same bitterness*; and, thirdly, I will ask you to notice that *this bitterness has most gracious effects upon us.*

Our First Sight of Christ Brings Bitterness into Our Soul

First, then, I want to point out to you that OUR FIRST SIGHT OF CHRIST BRINGS BITTERNESS INTO OUR SOUL. When a man, for the first time, by faith sees Christ upon the cross, and understands the meaning of His great substitutionary sacrifice, *he is bitterly grieved because he has not known Him before*. Imagine the case of a Jew who has, perhaps, lived in a nominally Christian country for fifty years. He has frequently heard the name of Jesus mentioned in various ways, but he has always received it with indignation, possibly even with ridicule. It is quite likely that he has spoken very bitter things against the Nazarene, repeating the old stories current among his race concerning the Prophet of Nazareth, and all the while thinking that he was doing service to Jehovah by rejecting one whom he supposed to be a pretender. Imagine that man, all of a sudden, convinced that Jesus of Nazareth is indeed the Son of God, the only Savior of sinners, the promised hope of Israel's seed. Why, I think, if there were not many sweet and precious thoughts to be mingled with the bitter ones, he would be almost driven to utter despair.

Surely he would, with humble penitence and many tears, fall down at the dear Savior's feet, and cry, "Forgive me, Lord, every opprobrious epithet that I have ever uttered; pardon me for every scornful word that I have spoken; forget every hard and cruel speech that I have made against You, O bleeding Lamb of God, whose blood takes away the sin of the world!"

I beseech some of you, who are not Jews, but sinners of the Gentiles, to recollect that your position is no better than theirs, and in some respects it is even worse. I know mine was, because I knew Jesus to be the Messiah. I never had a doubt about that, and yet I did not believe in Him. I acknowledged Him to be the Son of God. From my childhood I was taught that great truth and accepted it as a fact, yet I did not obey Him as my Lord and my God. I knew Him to be the only Savior of sinners, and if anyone had spoken contrary to that truth in my presence, my indignation would have burned against him; yet, all the while so far as my own consciousness was concerned, He was no Savior to me. I knew that He hung upon the cross that He might save the guilty, but I did not, for a long time, realize that I had a personal interest in His saving grace.

From my own experience, I am sure that the bitterness of anyone who has sinned in that way, when at last he understands the great plan of salvation, and finds that Christ loved him, and gave Himself to death for him, must be quite as great as the bitterness of the Jews who make the same discovery. For, lo, my brethren, they did it ignorantly in unbelief, but you and I have done it wantonly, or at least carelessly, and indifferently, knowing that we were rejecting our mother's Savior and our father's Christ. Herein is much of bitterness that you ought to feel, and when you do get a true view of Jesus as your Substitute and Savior, you will feel it very acutely, and you will say to yourself, "O, that I had known Him before! O, that I had loved Him before! O, that I had trusted Him before! Alas! that all these years should have been wasted, and that I should have chosen sin rather than the Savior, and the pleasures of the world sooner than the delights of His dear love." I know that you will have bitterness about that matter when you really come to Christ for salvation.

Next, there will come over your soul, when you get a true sight of Christ, much bitterness *on account of your having slighted the extraordinary love of Christ to you.* This truth will come home to your heart, with wonderful power, "He loved me, and gave Himself for me. For me He wore that crown of thorns, for me He endured that terrible scourging, for me He bore the piercing of those nails, for me He agonized unto that bloody sweat, for me He suffered even unto death." And then you will say, "And yet I have been all this while slighting Him! Others have loved me, and I have returned their love, ashamed to be thought ungrateful; but all of them put together have never loved me as He has done, yet I have been His enemy, and, as far as I could, I have opposed Him. He has stood outside my door, and knocked, and I have kept Him waiting there till His head has been filled with dew, and His locks with the drops of the night. Woe is me! Woe is me, that I should have treated so ill my best Friend!"

It is long, dear brothers and sisters, since my heart ceased to shut Him out. I admitted Him long ago; but even while I am talking to you about it, I feel all the old bitterness of that sad past coming over me. I could stand here and weep to think that, though I loved Him comparatively early in life, I did not love Him earlier, and did not sooner yield to His persistent knocking, and to the gracious pressure of His infinite love.

Another bitterness, which ought soon to be banished, steals over the heart; it is this, *the fear lest Christ should not be ours after all.* I have known some, who have understood the doctrine of the cross right well, and have believed in the great love of Jesus Christ for sinners; but then there has come over their mind and heart that dark doubting thought, "Will His blood be available for us? Will He ever be ours? After years of rejecting Him, shall we ever find Him, or have we forever missed Him? Is our day of grace past, or does He still wait to be gracious? Will He still accept us, or has He gone away, saying, 'I will give them up; they are joined unto idols, so I will let them alone'?"

O the bitterness of such a question as that! To see living water, clear as crystal, leaping up close by you, and yet to fear that you may not drink of it! To see the bread of life placed upon the table, and yet to doubt whether your unworthy lips may ever taste of that heavenly food! That is bitterness indeed; but let it be a bitterness that goes away at once and forever, for there is no question about that matter. If you will believe in Jesus, that is proof positive that God wills it. The question is never about God's will, when once your will is surrendered to Christ. If you are willing to accept Christ, it is because it is the day of God's power, and He has made you willing. If you will have Christ, He presents Himself to you with this gracious word, "Whosoever will, let him take the water of life freely." So let that bitter thought be nailed up to the cross, and die forever.

Then there follows, over and above all this, the black, bitter thought that *our sin caused His death on the tree.* The awakened soul sighs, "My sins! My sins! My sins!" Nothing ever reveals sin like the cross of Christ. Milton pictures Ithuriel with his spear touching the toad that lay squatting at Eve's ear, and suddenly it arose in the form of the dark fiend of hell. So does the cross touch what we thought to be only mistakes and errors, and they rise before us in their true character as hellish sins. In the light of Calvary, sin does like itself appear; and what is the likeness of sin there? Why, the murderer of the Son of God—the murderer of the Prince of Life—the murderer of man's best Friend, whose only crime was this: "found guilty of excess of love," and therefore He must die.

O sin, is this what you are? Are you a God-killing thing? I have heard of men being guilty of regicide; but what shall I say concerning Deicide? Yet sin virtually, and as much as it can, stabs at the Godhead, crying, with the wicked husbandmen, "This is the heir; come, let us kill him, and the inheritance shall be ours." This is the terrible character of sin—it will imbrue its hands in the blood of Him who is perfectly innocent and perfectly benevolent; it will take man's best Friend by the throat, condemn Him as if He were a felon, nail Him to a gibbet, and then stand and gaze at Him, and mock His very death-throes. There is nothing upon earth that is so devilish as sin. O to what extremes of atrocity has sin not gone!

And such is your sin and mine, to a greater or less degree. A sight of the cross, therefore, brings bitterness into the soul, because it shows us what sin is, and what are its ultimate issues and true designs if it could carry them out. Never do we smite upon our breast so hard as when we see the cross of Jesus. We are condemned at the mercy seat even more fully than we are at the judgment seat. This is the condemnation of sin in the soul of man, that he sees what it did in murdering the Christ of God, and this causes the repenting sinner to "be in bitterness for him, as one who is in bitterness for his firstborn."

To this is added another source of bitterness, namely, *the discovery of the wrath of God on account of sin.* You stand in imagination, and look at Jesus Christ dying upon the cross, and you say to yourself, "The Romans are here, and the Jews are here, and all men are here, representatively; but there is Someone greater than all these here." Then there comes to you from the ancient prophecy this message, "It pleased the Lord to bruise him; he hath put him to grief: when thou shalt make his soul an offering for sin, he shall see his seed, he shall prolong his days, and the pleasure of the Lord shall prosper in his hand." Yes, God Himself put Christ into the sinner's place through wondrous love to us, and as Christ stood in the sinner's place, though a sinner He could never be, God treated Him as if He were actually the sinner.

See how the Father's wrath burns against human sin; He could not be angry with His well-beloved Son; but, inasmuch as Christ stood in the Sinner's place, God poured out the vials of His wrath upon Him just as if He had been guilty. Behold how the Father smites Him; these are His words, "Awake, O sword." Will not the rod suffice, great God? No. "Awake, O sword, against my shepherd, and against the man that is my fellow, saith the Lord of hosts. Smite the shepherd." But will not some common smiting be sufficient? No; to the very heart He must be smitten, and Jesus must die the death of the cross that we may live forever.

How God must hate sin, then, and what wrath must fall upon me! That is the convicted sinner's thought. *My sin is personal and actual, and not, like Christ's, imputed; and since it is my own, how can God continue to bear with me?* And the dark suggestion comes into the soul, "He will not bear with you much longer, for it is written, 'I will ease me of mine adversaries.'" Yes, verily, a true sight of the cross makes us full of bitterness on account of the awful guilt of sin, and the divine wrath which it provokes.

And then comes the bitterness of *the dread of never being forgiven*. The convinced sinner says, "God spared not His only begotten Son when sin was laid upon Him; then, surely, He will not spare me. I am full of guilt, and I have within me a fountain of evil which is perpetually bubbling up with foulness—how can the pure and holy God spare me? Whither can I flee to get away from His presence? How can I escape from the bolts of His righteous wrath? Let me fly whither I may, He will pursue me, and overtake me, and destroy me."

Do any of you know what it is to feel like this? I remember when I did; I was in such terror that I feared lest every step I took should be my last, and that I should stumble first into my grave and then into hell. "Did the cross make you feel like that?" you ask. Yes, certainly; for I could not but think that, though Jesus cried, "My God, my God, why hast thou forsaken me?" I should never have to ask that question, because I should know why God had forsaken me, for my sin was sufficient to drive Him away from me forever.

I feel quite sure that God intends our first sight of Christ to fill our soul with bitterness; and therefore I ask you most seriously to question your conversion unless there was some measure of this bitterness mingled with it. A sinner's sight of Christ must breed sorrow for sin; it is unavoidable; and the more clear that sight shall become, and the more it is mixed with faith, and the more sure we are of pardon, the more bitterness will there be in it. When we know that our sins are forgiven, it is then that we most of all realize their guilt, and abhor and hate them. That hymn which we sometimes sing exactly sets forth this truth—

> My sins, my sins, my Savior,
>   How sad on Thee they fall!
> Seen through Thy gentle patience,
>   I tenfold feel them all.
>
> I know they are forgiven,
>   But still their pain to me
> Is all the grief and anguish
>   They laid, my Lord, on Thee.

My sins, my sins, my Savior!
Their guilt I never knew
Till, with Thee, in the desert
I near Thy passion drew;

Till with Thee in the garden
I heard Thy pleading prayer,
And saw the sweat-drops bloody
That told Thy sorrow there.

Our Continued Sight of Christ Works in Us a Measure of the Same Bitterness

Now, secondly, OUR CONTINUED SIGHT OF CHRIST WORKS IN US A MEA-
SURE OF THE SAME BITTERNESS. For, first, *as the great love of Christ is better
known, it brings deeper grief for sin.* We then more deeply lament that we
should ever have slighted such love, and that such love should ever have
been called to so vast a sacrifice as that which it made for us. I do not suppose, beloved, that your knowledge of the love of Christ at first was at all
comparable to what it is now; if you have studied in the school of Christ's
love, and have believed it to be the most excellent of all the sciences, you
will, by the teaching of the Spirit, and by experience, attain a clearer
knowledge of the love of Christ which passes knowledge; and side by side
with that will be a growing sense of abhorrence of yourself, and detesta-
tion of the sin which nailed your Savior to the tree. It must be so; deeper
love to Christ will breed greater grief and a yet more bitter bitterness on
account of sin.

There will also be, in your heart, a more intense bitterness arising from
the dread of grieving your Lord. O have you not sometimes wished that
you could die rather than run any risk of apostasy?

I marvel not at the poor Methodist who, when surrounded by blasphemers, who seemed as if they would drive him from Christ, fell on his
knees, and prayed the Lord to take him home to heaven, so that he might
never again be tempted to go astray. Bitterer than death itself would it be
for us ever to dishonor that dear name by which we are called. Feel you not
so, my brother, my sister? I believe that, the higher your joy in Christ, the
greater will be your fear lest you should bring disgrace upon Him. You
stand almost on the top of the mountain of communion, you seem to be
transfigured with your Master, and to be glowing with the light that streams
from Him; yet even there the thought comes to you, *What if, after all this,
I should slip with my feet? Peter, who was one of the three with the Lord
on the holy mount, himself afterward denied his Master with oaths and
curses; then, may not I also be found wanting in the time of trial?* This self-
examination is almost needful to the mellowing of our holy joy.

As the sycamore fig never ripens till it is bruised, so there is a high joy of fellowship that needs bruising, by a sense of our own weakness, ere its essential sweetness shall be fully developed. I have a great fear concerning your condition if you never felt anything of this bitterness—this dread lest, in thought, or word, or deed, by omission or by commission, you should grieve the sweet and tender love of Christ. You know how the spouse said, "I charge you, ye daughters of Jerusalem, by the roes, and by the hinds of the field"—by all that is most gentle, and timid, and delicate, and jealous, and full of love—"that ye stir not up, nor awake my love, till he please." It is thus that the holy soul feels the bitterness of an inward jealousy lest she should be treacherous to her Lord, or that anything should occur to grieve Him.

The next bitterness is caused by *a deeper regret on account of our own unworthiness*. I think that those who love Christ much, and who have had a clear view of His love, never can be satisfied with themselves. Do you ever rise from your knees, and say, "I am quite content with that prayer"? If so, I fancy that you cannot have prayed "with groanings which cannot be uttered." Did you ever preach a sermon, brother, and feel, after it was finished, that you could run up the top-gallants, and cry, "Never man preached as I have done"? If so, I am afraid that it was very poor preaching, with many fine feathers in its tail to spread out like a peacock's, but with few feathers in its wings to make it mount up like an eagle. It will never do for us to be satisfied with ourselves, for vehement love thinks nothing good enough for Christ. When it reaches its best, it says, "My best is utter poverty compared with His deserts."

"Oh!" says the saint who truly loves His Lord, "I am ashamed to bring Him even my best offerings; and when, sometimes, I lie at His feet, and feel that I am perfectly consecrated, I still wish that there was something better to consecrate, and that I could keep up that complete consecration at all times and seasons, and under all circumstances." But since it is not so with any one of us, there is a bitterness that mingles with the very sight of Christ. You may look at yourself until you get quite pleased with yourself, but you cannot remain so when once you look at Him.

You know how Job spoke to the Lord, when he took his right position before Him, "I have heard of thee by the hearing of the ear: but now mine eye seeth thee. Wherefore I abhor myself, and repent in dust and ashes." Those who think themselves perfect had better come and look at their Lord; and then, if their comeliness is not turned to corruption, I shall be greatly mistaken. A glimpse at Him would act like flames of fire turning dry stubble into ashes; for, in a moment, all their glory would be utterly consumed.

Then, again, I am sure there is another bitterness that will always accompany a true sight of Christ, and that is, *an intense horror at man's rejection of Him.* Have not you, beloved, sometimes looked at your Lord, and loved and adored Him, till, first, you have pitied men, and afterward you have pitied Christ? With those who love Christ most, there comes to be, after a time, sympathy with Jesus rather than with men. I can understand how, even when the enemies of God shall be destroyed at the last, and the smoke of their torment shall rise up forever and ever, the perfect ones in heaven will sing, "Hallelujah." Certain persons, who are on earth at the present time, if they had been at the Red Sea, and seen old Pharaoh's army cast into the depths, would have mournfully said, "This is very, very grievous to us."

But as for me, if I had been there, I would have joined with Moses and with Miriam, and said, "Sing ye to the Lord, for he hath triumphed gloriously; the horse and his rider hath he thrown into the sea." I confess that I have very small sympathy with Pharaoh, but I have the most intense sympathy with Jehovah and with His people; and I question whether the wonderful sympathy with lost sinners, which some people profess to feel, is not sympathy with their sin as much as with themselves, perhaps unconsciously to those who indulge it.

If we were perfectly holy, we should desire to do just what God does, and we should wish God to do exactly what He is doing, and we should rejoice without question in all the will of God. One result of such a state of mind as that would be that we should cry with the psalmist, "Horror hath taken hold upon me because of the wicked that forsake thy law." I do not know that I ever felt a greater horror in my soul than when, in Rome, I stood at the foot of the Santa Scala—"the holy staircase," as they call it— on which they pretend to show the marks where our Savior fainted on the stairs in Jerusalem. I saw poor deluded creatures go up and down those stairs upon their knees, repeating certain forms of prayer all the while. Ah, me! it did seem horrible; and, worst of all, the priests have turned the Christ Himself into an idol. There is a little black picture of Him, at the top of the stairs, which is reputed to have been painted by Luke, and it is kissed and worshiped, and thus even our blessed Master is made to act the lackey to idolatry. I thought that, if I could have borrowed a thunderbolt or two for a little while, I could have made a clean sweep here and there in Rome; but the time for that is not yet. That time will come, and a very clean sweep there will be when the cry is heard, "Babylon the great is fallen, is fallen. . . . And her smoke rose up forever and ever."

But, brethren, there is an intense bitterness in your heart when you come truly to see Christ on the cross, as you realize that all people do not believe in Him, that His kingdom has not yet come, and that His will is not done on earth as it is in heaven. Still do men reject Him; they scoff at His gospel, they despise His cause, they set up idol gods and false saviors, and all this is as a dish of bitter herbs to those who really love Him. It seems passing strange that He should ever have entered into this awful battle between good and evil, that He should have come, the foremost and noblest of champions, baring His arm for the war, and that in the fight He should not only have sweat as it were great drops of blood, but that He should have had His heart broken in the fray.

Ah, me! how sad it is that He whom angels worship, and in whom God Himself delights, should be trampled by the feet of wicked men, like mire in the streets; that they should dare to defile with their spittle that face which outshines the sun, and pour contempt and scorn upon Him who fills eternity with the splendors of the Deity! All this is like bitter herbs to those who love Him. Still, the final victory will be won by Him, and it will be worth all that it costs. Up the everlasting hills He has already ascended, victor from the fight; and today He divides the spoil with the strong. But, O, that it had been possible for that bitter cup to have passed from Him! O, that it had been possible that He should not drink the hell-draught! Yet He did drink it to the last dregs; it is all over now, glory be to His holy name! But the taste of the bitter herbs is always present with the true Paschal Lamb to those who spiritually feed thereon by faith.

This Bitterness Has Most Gracious Effects upon Us

Now I must close by noticing that THIS BITTERNESS HAS MOST GRACIOUS EFFECTS UPON US. First, it must be evident to you all that *this bitterness works great hatred of sin.* We see how cruel sin has been to Christ, and we therefore seek to avoid it. The burnt child dreads the fire; but we are not quite in that condition. We dread the fire of sin because it burned the Savior; that is why we hate it so intensely. Sin murdered Him; so, can we ever tolerate it? Could anyone ever play with the knife that had killed his best friend? Could he preserve it as a choice treasure? Nay, he would, if he could, fling it into the depths of oblivion; and sin, that cruel murderous thing that slew our Savior, we would take revenge upon you! We abhor you; God has made you bitter to us; and there dwells, in that bitterness, a power that helps to sanctify us.

But next, *that bitterness makes Christ very sweet.* "Why!" you ask, "how is that?" Well, I suppose that the bitter herbs made the paschal lamb taste all the sweeter to the Israelite of old; and I am sure that a bitter sense of sin, and bitter regrets that we should ever have cost our Savior so much, and a bitter sense of our own unworthiness, all make Christ more precious to us. It is like the two balances in a pair of scales; when you go up, Christ goes down; and when you go down, down, down, down, to nothing, and far below zero, then Christ goes up. No man can know the sweetness of Christ who has not tasted the bitterness of sin.

Next, *it makes all worldly things lose their taste.* If you get some of the bitterness that comes of mourning about Christ, the sweetest things of the world will have but very little attraction for you. I will give you an illustration of this truth. Suppose you had an only son, and that you lost him; would not everything look dark about you then? It comes home to a man's heart very heavily when such a treasure is taken away from him. He has a farm, but he has no joy in it, the old home seems to be a very dreary place to him now; he wishes to move away from it, and to forget all it contained. That is the kind of bitterness of which our text speaks: "They shall mourn for him, as one mourneth for his only son, and shall be in bitterness for him, as one that is in bitterness for his firstborn." And thus the world loses its charms for true believers, as Paul says, "It remaineth, that both they that have wives be as though they had none; and they that weep, as though they wept not; and they that rejoice, as though they rejoiced not," because a stronger flavor has taken possession of their palate, and made them forget everything else. Thus, the bitterness of mourning for Christ takes away the power to enjoy the sweets of this world.

But there is something better than that, for *it removes the bitterness from the things of this life*. Suppose you suffer great pain. I was yesterday by the side of a dear sister in Christ who has undergone terrible pain, and she said to me, "Thoughts of the Lord Jesus, and of His sufferings, were so sweet to me that I seemed only to recollect my own griefs as they helped me to remember His." That is how it should be with each of us; as we are called to suffer, we should say—

> His way was much rougher and darker than mine;
> Did Christ, my Lord, suffer, and shall I repine?

How often the bitterness of poverty has vanished when men have thought of Him who had not where to lay His head! How frequently the bitterness of persecution has departed when His followers have remembered that He was despised and rejected of men; a man of sorrows, and acquainted with grief! One brings us what he says is a bitter draught, and we say, "Do you call that bitter? I have tasted something much more bitter than that; I can drink it, and even rejoice in it, since I have been taught how to take the very gall of bitterness, that which has the intensity of the bitterest Peruvian bark, even sympathy with my Savior in His awful sufferings."

And let me also tell you, dear brethren, that one effect of this bitterness upon the soul that feels it is, *to take away all bitterness against your fellow-men*. If you have really felt the bitterness of your sin against Christ, you have said to yourself, "Well, now, after this, I must be sweet, and gentle, and kind, and tender, and forgiving toward others. Somebody has offended me. Ah, but then how much I offended God! He will not ask my forgiveness, he says. Yes, but my Lord prayed for those who put Him to death, and said, 'Father, forgive them,' though they sought not forgiveness;

must not I do the same?" I am sure that, if you mourn on account of your own sin, you will be the last person in the world to be harsh and severe in your judgment upon others. You will say, "I cannot take up the stone to cast at them, even if others do so."

The poor harlot comes before the Savior, and the self-righteous Pharisees will accuse her; but no one of us, I think, will do so, for who among us has not been guilty; and if we have been pardoned, how can we condemn others? I charge any of you, who harbor ill-will against others, to remember that you cannot be Christians if you carry that foul serpent in your bosom. You can bring no acceptable sacrifices to God's altar while you are at enmity against your brother. "He that loveth not his brother whom he hath seen, how can he love God whom he hath not seen?" Whatever else you may or may not do, this you must do, forgive as you would be forgiven; and let the bitterness of your sympathy with Christ take away from your nature all bitterness, and harshness, and unkindness, and malice, toward your fellow-men.

Last of all, *in this bitterness with Christ, there is an unutterable sweetness.* If I were asked when I have felt most happy, if the question were put to me in the most unlimited sense, "When did you feel such happiness as you could wish always to feel?"—I should not quote any of the days of earth's mirth, for, as the crackling of thorns under a pot, so is the best of mortal merriment. I could not even quote the day in which I first knew the Lord, because, though there was an intensity of delight about it, it was not so deep as the joy I am going to mention. Neither, if I had to ask for a joy that might continue with me, should I ask to have the high delights which I have often experienced when in sweetest fellowship with my Lord, for that kind of joy is killing; we cannot endure much of it. But I think that the sweetest joy I ever felt was when, racked with pain, and broken all asunder, I fell back upon the omnipotent love of God, like a child who cannot walk, or move, or even stand, but just lies on its mother's breast, quite passive, quite at peace.

I think that mourning for sin is as sweet a flower as blooms outside heaven. I suppose that pearl of flowers blooms not on the other side of Jordan. It is the only flower on earth that I would like to carry there, just as Rowland Hill used to say that repentance and he had kept such sweet company that the only regret he had about heaven was that he supposed he should not repent there. Well, all that is good, we shall have there; "and there shall in no wise enter into it anything that defileth." But I do assure you, from my own experience, that the still, calm, quiet joy which does not well up out of yourself, but comes into you direct from Christ by the way of the cross—that dew which falls not on Hermon, but on Calvary—is the rarest and most roseate dew that ever charms us this side of the glory-land. God give you all to know, to the full extent, the sweet bitterness—the bitter sweetness—that comes of a sight of Christ crucified, for His dear name's sake! Amen.

9

*Up from the Country and Pressed into Service**

And they compel one Simon a Cyrenian, who passed by, coming out of the country, the father of Alexander and Rufus, to bear his cross (Mark 15:21).

John tells us that our Savior went forth bearing His cross (John 19:17). We are much indebted to John for inserting that fact. The other evangelists mention Simon the Cyrenian as hearing the cross of Christ; but John, who often fills up gaps which are left by the other three, tells us that Jesus set out to Calvary carrying His own cross. Our Lord Jesus came out from Pilate's palace laden with His cross, but He was so extremely emaciated and so greatly worn by the night of the bloody sweat, that the procession moved too slowly for the rough soldiers, and therefore they took the cross from their prisoner and laid it upon Simon; or possibly they laid the long end upon the shoulder of the strong countryman, while the Savior still continued to bear in part His cross till He came to the place of doom.

It is well that we should be told that the Savior bore His cross; for if it had not been so, objectors would have had ground for disputation. I hear them say: You admit that one of the most prominent types, in the Old Testament, of the sacrifice of the Son of God, was Abraham's offering up his son Isaac; now, Abraham laid the wood upon Isaac his son, and not upon a servant. Should not therefore the Son of God bear the cross Himself? Had not our Lord carried His cross, there would have been a flaw in His fulfillment of the type ; therefore, the Savior must bear the wood when He goes forth to be offered up as a sacrifice.

One of the greatest of English preachers has well reminded us that the fulfillment of this type appeared to have been in eminent jeopardy, since,

* This sermon was preached on Sunday morning, August 2, 1885, at the Metropolitan Tabernacle, Newington, and is taken from *The Metropolitan Tabernacle Pulpit.*

at the very first, our Lord's weakness must have been apparent, and the reason which led to the laying of the cross upon the Cyrenian might have prevented our Lord's carrying the cross at all. If the soldiers had a little earlier put the cross upon Simon, which they might very naturally have done, then the prophecy had not been fulfilled; but God has the minds of men so entirely at His control, that even in the minutest circumstances He can order all things so as to complete the merest jots and tittles of the prophecy. Our Lord was made to be, in all points, an Isaac, and therefore we see Him going forth bearing the wood of the burnt-offering. Thus you see that it was important that Jesus should for a while bear His own cross.

But it was equally instructive that someone else should be made a partaker of the burden ; for it has always been part of the divine counsel that for the salvation of men from sin the Lord should be associated with His church. So far as atonement is concerned, the Lord has trodden the wine press alone, and of the people there was none with Him; but as far as the conversion of the world is concerned, and its rescue from the power of error and wickedness, Christ is not alone. We are workers together with God. We are ourselves to be in the hands of God part bearers of the sorrow and travail by which men are to be delivered from the bondage of sin and Satan, and brought into the liberty of truth and righteousness. Hence it became important that in the bearing of the cross, though not in the death upon it, there should be yoked with the Christ one who should follow close behind Him.

To bear the cross after Jesus is the office of the faithful. Simon the Cyrenian is the representative of the whole church of God, and of each believer in particular. Often had Jesus said, "Except a man take up his cross daily, and follow me, he cannot be my disciple"; and now at last He embodies that sermon in an actual person. The disciple must be as his Master: he that would follow the Crucified must himself bear the cross: this we see visibly set forth in Simon of Cyrene with the cross of Jesus laid upon his shoulder.

> Shall Simon bear the cross alone,
> And all the rest go free?
> No; there's a cross for every one
> And there's a cross for me.

The lesson to each one of us is to take up our Lord's cross without delay, and go with Him, without the camp, bearing His reproach. That many among this vast and mixed congregation may imitate Simon is the anxious desire of my heart. With holy expectancy I gaze upon this throng collected from all parts of the earth, and I long to find in it some who will take my Lord's yoke upon them this day.

Unexpected Persons Are Often Called to Cross-Bearing

I will begin with this first remark, that UNEXPECTED PERSONS ARE OFTEN CALLED TO CROSS-BEARING. Like Simon, they are impressed into the service of Christ. Our text says: "They compel one Simon a Cyrenian, who passed by, coming out of the country, the father of Alexander and Rufus, to bear his cross." Simon did not volunteer, but was forced into this work of cross-bearing. It would seem from another evangelist that he speedily yielded to the impressment, and lifted the burden heartily; but at first he was compelled. A rude authority was exercised by the guard; who being upon the Governor's business acted with high-handed rigor, and forced whomsoever they pleased to do their bidding. By the exercise of such irresponsible power they compelled a passing stranger to carry Christ's cross. It was specially singular that the man to have this honor was not Peter, nor James, nor John, nor any one of the many who had for years listened to the Redeemer's speech; but it was a stranger from Northern Africa, who bad been in no way connected with the life or teachings of Jesus of Nazareth.

Notice, first, that *he was an unknown man.* He was spoken of "as one Simon." Simon was a very common name among the Jews, almost as common as John in our own country. This man was just "one Simon"—an individual who need not be further described. But the providence of God had determined that this obscure individual, this certain man, or I might better say, this uncertain man, should be selected to the high office of cross-bearer to the Son of God. I have an impression upon my mind that there is "one Simon" here this morning, who has to bear Christ's cross from this time forward. I feel persuaded that I am right. That person is so far unknown that most probably he does not recognize a single individual in all this throng, neither does anybody in this assembly know anything of *him*: certainly the preacher does not. He is one John, one Thomas, or one William ; or perhaps, in the feminine, she is one Mary, one Jane, one Maggie. Friend, nobody knows you save our Father who is in heaven, and He has appointed you to have fellowship with His Son. I shall roughly describe you as "one Simon," and leave the Holy Spirit to bring you into your place and service.

But this "one Simon" was a very particular *"one* Simon." I lay the emphasis where there might seem to be no need of any: he was one whom God knew, and chose, and loved, and set apart for this special service. In a congregation like the present, there may be somebody whom our God intends to use for His glory during the rest of his life. That person sits in the pew and listens to what I am saying, and perhaps as yet he does not begin to inquire whether he is that "one Simon," that one person; and yet it is so, and ere this sermon is ended, he shall know that the call to bear the cross is for him.

Many more unlikely things than this have happened in this house of prayer. I pray that many a man may go out from this house a different man from the man he was when He entered it an hour ago. That man Saul, that great persecutor of the church, afterward became such a mighty preacher of the gospel that people exclaimed with wonder, "There is a strange alteration in this man." "Why," said one, "when I knew him he was a Pharisee of the Pharisees. He was as bigoted a man as ever wore a phylactery, and he hated Christ and Christians so intensely that he could never persecute the Church sufficiently." "Yes," replied another, "it was so; but he has had a strange twist. They say that he was going down to Damascus to hunt out the disciples, and something happened; we do not know exactly what it was, but evidently it gave him such a turn that he has never been himself since. In fact, he seems turned altogether upside down, and the current of his life is evidently reversed: he lives enthusiastically for that faith which once he destroyed." This speedy change happened to "one Saul of Tarsus."

There were plenty of Sauls in Israel, but upon this one Saul electing love had looked in the counsels of eternity; for that Saul redeeming love had shed its heart's blood; and in that Saul effectual grace wrought mightily. Is there another Saul here today? The Lord grant that he may now cease to kick against the pricks, and may we soon hear of him, "Behold he prayeth." I feel convinced the counterpart of that "one Simon" is in this house at this moment, and my prayer goes up to God, and I hope it is attended with the prayers of many thousands besides, that he may at once submit to the Lord Jesus.

It did not seem likely that Simon should bear the cross of Christ, for *he was a stranger who had newly come up from the country*. He probably knew little or nothing of what had been taking place in Jerusalem; for he had come from another continent. He was "one Simon a Cyrenian"; and I suppose that Cyrene could not have been less than 800 miles from Jerusalem. It was situated in what is now called Tripoli, in Northern Africa, in which place a colony of Jews had been formed long before. Very likely he had come in a Roman galley from Alexandria to Joppa, and there had been rowed through the surf, and landed in time to reach Jerusalem for the Passover. He had long wanted to come to Jerusalem; he had heard the fame of the temple and of the city of his fathers; and he had longed to see the great Assembly of the tribes, and the solemn Paschal feast. He had traveled all those miles, he had hardly yet got the motion of the ship out of his brain, and it had never entered into his head that he should be impressed by the Roman guard, and made to assist at an execution.

It was a singular providence that he should come into the city at the moment of the turmoil about Jesus, and should have crossed the street just as the sad procession started on its way to Golgotha. He passed by neither too soon nor too late; he was on the spot as punctually as if he had made an appointment to be there; and yet, as men speak, it was all by mere chance. I cannot tell how many providences had worked together to bring him there at the nick of time, but so the Lord would have it, and so it came about. He, a man there in Cyrene, in Northern Africa, must at a certain date, at the tick of the clock, be at Jerusalem, in order that he might help to carry the cross up to Mount Calvary; *and he was there.* Ah! my dear friend, I do not know what providences have been at work to bring you here today; perhaps very strange ones. If a little something had occurred you had not taken this journey; it only needed a small dust to turn the scale, and you would have been hundreds of miles from this spot, in quite another scene from this. Why you are here you do not yet know, except that you have come to listen to the preacher, and join the throng. But God knows why He has brought you here. I trust it will be read in the annals of the future:

> Thus the eternal mandate ran,
> Almighty grace arrest that man.

God has brought you here, that on this spot, by the preaching of the gospel, you may be compelled to bear the cross of Jesus. I pray it may be so. "One Simon a Cyrenian, coming out of the country," is here after a long journey, and this day he will begin to live a higher and a better life.

Further, notice, *Simon had come for another purpose.* He had journeyed to Jerusalem with no thought of bearing the cross of Jesus. Probably Simon was a Jew far removed from the land of his fathers, and he had made a pilgrimage to the holy city to keep the Passover. Every Jew loved to be present at Jerusalem at the Paschal feast. So, to put it roughly, it was holiday-time; it was a time for making an excursion to the capital; it was a season for making a journey and going up to the great city which was "beautiful for situation, the joy of the whole earth." Simon from far-off Cyrene must by all means keep the feast at Jerusalem. Perhaps he had saved his money for months, that he might pay his fare to Joppa; and he had counted down the gold freely for the joy which he had in going to the city of David, and the temple of his God.

He was come for the Passover, and for that only; and he would be perfectly satisfied to go home when once the feast was over, and once he had partaken of the lamb with the tribes of Israel. Then he could say throughout the rest of his life, "I, too, was once at the great feast of our people, when we commemorated the coming up out of Egypt." Brethren, we propose one way, but God has other propositions. We say, "I will step in and hear the preacher," but God means that the arrows of His grace shall stick fast in our hearts. Many and many a time with no desire for grace men have listened to the gospel, and the Lord has been found of them that sought Him not.

I heard of one who cared little for the sermon till the preacher chanced to use that word "eternity" and the hearer was taken prisoner by holy thoughts, led to the Savior's feet. Men have stepped into places of worship even with evil designs, and yet the purpose of grace has been accomplished; they came to scoff, but they remained to pray. Some have been cast by the providence of God into positions where they have met with Christian men, and a word of admonition has been blessed to them.

A lady was one day at an evening party, and there met with Cæsar Malan, the famous divine of Geneva, who, in his usual manner, inquired of her whether she was a Christian. She was startled, surprised, and vexed, and made a short reply to the effect that it was not a question she cared to discuss; whereupon, Mr. Malan replied with great sweetness that he would not persist in *speaking* of it, but he would pray that she might be led to give her heart to Christ, and become a useful worker for Him. Within a fortnight she met the minister again, and asked him how she must come to Jesus. Mr. Malan's reply was, "Come to Him just as you are." That lady gave herself up to Jesus: it was Charlotte Elliott, to whom we owe that precious hymn—

> Just as I am—without one plea
> But that Thy blood was shed for me,
> And that Thou bidd'st me come to Thee—
> O Lamb of God, I come.

It was a blessed thing for her that she was at that party, and that the servant of God from Geneva should have been there, and should have spoken to her so faithfully. O for many a repetition of the story "of one Simon a Cyrenian," coming, not with the intent to bear the cross, but with quite another mind, and yet being enlisted in the cross-bearing army of the Lord Jesus!

I would have you notice, once more, that this man was at this particular time not thinking upon the subject at all, for *he was at that time merely passing by.* He had come up to Jerusalem, and whatever occupied his mind he does not appear to have taken any notice of the trial of Jesus, or of the sad end of it. It is expressly said that he "passed by." He was not even sufficiently interested in the matter to stand in the crowd and look at the mournful procession. Women were weeping there right bitterly—the daughters of Jerusalem to whom the Master said, "Weep not for me, but weep for yourselves, and for your children"; but this man passed by. He was anxious to hurry away from so unpleasant a sight, and to get up to the temple. He was quietly making his way through the crowd, eager to go about his business, and he must have been greatly surprised and distressed when a rough hand was laid upon him, and a stern voice said, "Shoulder that cross."

There was no resisting a Roman centurion when he gave a command, and so the countryman meekly submitted, wishing, no doubt, that he were back in Cyrene tilling the ground. He must needs stoop his shoulder and take up a new burden, and tread in the footsteps of the mysterious personage to whom the cross belonged. He was only passing by, and yet he was enlisted and impressed by the Romans, and, as I take it, impressed by the grace of God for life; for whereas Mark says he was the father of Alexander and Rufus, it would seem that his sons were well-known to the Christian people to whom Mark was writing. If his son was the same Rufus that Paul mentions, then he calls her "his mother and mine"; and it would seem that Simon's wife and his sons became believers and partakers of the sufferings of Christ.

His contact with the Lord in that strange compulsory way probably wrought out for him another and more spiritual contact which made him a true cross-bearer. O you that pass by this day, draw nigh to Jesus! I have no wish to call your attention to myself, far from it; but I do ask your attention to my Lord. Though you only intended to slip into this tabernacle and slip out again, I pray that you may be arrested by a call from my Lord. I speak as my Lord's servant, and I would constrain you to come to Him. Stand where you are a while, and let me beg you to yield to His love, which even now would cast the bands of a man around you. I would compel you, by my Lord's authority, to take up His cross and bear it after Him. It would be strange, say you. Aye, so it might be, but it would be a glorious event.

I remember Mr. Knill, speaking of his own conversion, used an expression which I should like to use concerning one of you. Here it is: "It was just a quarter past twelve, August 2nd, when twang went every harp in Paradise; for a sinner had repented." May it be so with you. O that every harp in Paradise may now ring out the high praises of sovereign grace, as you now yield yourself to the great Shepherd and Bishop of souls! May that divine impressment which is imaged in the text by the compulsion of the Roman soldier take place in your case at this very moment; and may it be seen in your instance that unexpected persons are often called to be cross-bearers!

Cross-bearing Can Still Be Practiced

My second observation is—CROSS-BEARING CAN STILL BE PRACTICED. Very briefly let me tell you in what ways the cross can still be carried:

First, and chiefly, *by your becoming a Christian.* If the cross shall take you up, you will take up the cross. Christ will be your hope, His death your trust, Himself the object of your love. You never become a cross-bearer truly till you lay your burdens down at His feet who bore the cross and curse for you.

Next, you become a cross-bearer *when you make an open avowal of the Lord Jesus Christ.* Do not deceive yourselves—this is expected of each one of you if you are to be saved. The promise as I read it in the New Testament is not to the believer alone, but to the believer who confesses his faith. "He that with his heart believeth and with his mouth maketh confession of him shall be saved." He says, " He that confesseth me before men, him will I confess before my Father; but he that denieth me"—and from the connection it should seem to mean, he that does not confess Me— "him will I deny before my Father which is in heaven." To quote the inspired Scripture, "He that believeth and is baptized shall be saved."

There should be, there must be, the open avowal in Christ's own way of the secret faith which you have in Him. Now this is often a cross. Many people would like to go to heaven by an underground railway; secrecy suits them. They do not want to cross the channel; the sea is too rough; but when there is a tunnel made they will go to the fair country. My good people, you are cowardly, and I must quote to you a text which ought to sting your cowardice out of you: "But the fearful and unbelieving shall have their part in the lie which burneth with fire and brimstone." I say no more, and make no personal applications; but, I beseech you, run no risks. Be afraid to be afraid. Be ashamed of being ashamed of Christ. Shame on that man who counts it any shame to say before assembled angels, and men, and devils, "I am a follower of Christ." May you who have hitherto been secret followers of the crucified Lord become manifest cross-bearers! Do you not even now cry out, "Set down my name, sir"?

Further, some have to take up their cross by *commencing Christian work.* You live in a village where there is no gospel preaching: preach yourself. You are in a backwoods town where the preaching is very far from being such as God approves of: begin to preach the truth yourself. "Alas!" say you, "I should make a fool of myself." Are you ashamed to be a fool for Christ? "O, but I should break down." Break down: it will do you good, and perhaps you may break somebody else down. There is no better preaching in the world than that of a man who breaks down under a sense of unworthiness: if that breakdown communicates itself to other people, it may begin a revival.

If you are choked by your earnestness others may become earnest too. Do you still murmur, "But I should get the ill-will of everybody"? For Christ's sake could you not bear that? When the good monk said to Martin Luther, "Go thou home to thy cell and keep quiet," why did not Martin take the advice? Why, indeed? "It is very bad for young people to be so forward; you will do a great deal of mischief, therefore be quiet, you Martin. Who are you to interfere with the great authorities? Be holy for yourself, and don't trouble others. If you stir up a reformation, thousands of good people will be burnt through you. Do be quiet." Bless God, Martin did not go home, and was not quiet, but went about his Master's business, and raised heaven and earth by his brave witness-bearing.

Where are you, Martin, this morning? I pray God to call you out, and as you have confessed His name, and are His servant, I pray that He may make you bear public testimony for Him, and tell out the saving power of the Savior's precious blood. Come, Simon, I see you shrink; but the cross has to be carried; therefore bow your back. It is only a wooden cross, after all, and not an iron one. You can bear it: you must bear it. God help you.

Perhaps, too, some brother may have to take up his cross by *bearing witness against the rampant sin which surrounds him.* "Leave all those dirty matters alone; do not say a word about them. Let the people go to the devil, or else you will soil your white kid gloves." Sirs, we will spoil our hands as well as our gloves, and we will risk our characters, if need be; but we will put down the devilry which now defiles London. Truly the flesh does shrink, and the purest part of our manhood shrinks with it, when we are compelled to bear open protest against sins which are done of men in secret. But, Simon, the Master may yet compel you to bear His cross in this respect, and if so, He will give you both courage and wisdom, and your labor shall not be in vain in the Lord.

Sometimes, however, the cross-bearing is of another and more quiet kind, and may be described as *submission to providence.* A young friend is saying, "For me to live at home I know to be my duty; but father is unkind, and the family generally impose upon me. I wish I could get away." Ah! dear sister, you must bear Christ's cross, and it may be the Lord would have you remain at home. Therefore bear the cross. A servant is saying, "I should like to be in a Christian family. I do not think I can stop where I am." Perhaps, good sister, the Lord has put you where you are to be a light in a dark place. All the lamps should not be in one street, or what will become of the courts and alleys?

It is often the duty of a Christian to say, "I shall stop where I am and fight this matter through. I mean by character and example, with kindness and courtesy and love, to win this place for Jesus." Of course, the easy way is to turn monk and live quietly in a cloister, and serve God by doing nothing; or to turn nun and dwell in a convent, and expect to win the battle of life by running out of it. Is not this absurd? If you shut yourself away from this poor world, what is to become of it? You men and women who are Christians must stand up and stand out for Jesus where the providence of God has cast you: if your calling is not a sinful one, and if the temptations around you are not too great for you, you must "hold the fort" and never dream of surrender. If your lot is hard, look upon it as Christ's cross, and bow your back to the load. Your shoulder may be raw at first, but you will grow stronger before long, for as your day your strength shall be. "It is good for a man that he bear the yoke in his youth"; but it is good for a man to bear the cross in his old age as well as in his youth; in fact, we ought never to be quit of so blessed a burden. What wings are to a bird, and sails to a ship, that the cross becomes to a man's spirit when he fully consents to accept it as his life's beloved load. Truly did Jesus say, "My yoke is easy, and my burden is light." Now, Simon, where are you? Shoulder the cross, man, in the name of God!

To Cross-bearing There Are Noble Compulsions

Thirdly, TO CROSS-BEARING THERE ARE NOBLE COMPULSIONS. Simon's compulsion was the rough hand of the Roman legionary, and the gruff voice in the Latin tongue, "Shoulder that cross"; but we hear gentler voices which compel us this day to take up Christ's cross.

The first compulsion is this—*"the love of Christ constraineth us."* He has done all this for you; therefore by sweet but irresistible compulsion you are made to render Him some return of love. Does not Jesus appear to you in a vision as you sit in this house? Do you not see that thorn-crowned head, that visage crimsoned with the bloody sweat, those hands and feet pierced with the nails? Does He not say to you pointedly, "I did all this for thee; what hast thou done for me"? Startled in your seat, you cover your face, and inwardly reply, "I will answer that question by the rest of my life. I will be first and foremost a servant of Jesus: not a trader first and a Christian next, but a Christian first and a businessman afterward." You, my sister, must say, "I will live for Christ as a daughter, a wife, or a mother. I will live for my Lord; for He has given Himself for me, and I am not my own, but bought with a price."

The true heart will feel a compulsion arising from a second reflection, namely, *the glory of a life spent for God and for His Christ.* What is the life of a man who toils in business, makes money, becomes rich, and dies? It winds up with a paragraph in the *Illustrated London News*, declaring that he died worth so much: the wretch was not worth anything himself; his estate had value, he had none. Had he been worth anything he would have sent his money about the world doing good; but as a worthless steward he has laid his Master's stores in heaps to rot. The life of multitudes of men is self-seeking. It is ill for a man to live the life of swine. What a poor creature is the usual ordinary man! But a life spent for Jesus, though it involve cross-bearing, is noble, heroic, sublime. The mere earthworm leads a dunghill life. A life of what is called pleasure is a mean, beggarly business. A life of keeping up respectability is utter slavery—as well be a horse in a pug-mill. A life wholly consecrated to Christ and His cross is life indeed; it is akin to the life of angels; aye, higher still, it is the life of God within the soul of man. O you who have a spark of true nobility, seek to live lives worth living, worth remembering, worthy to be the commencement of eternal life before the throne of God.

Some of you ought to feel the cross coming upon your shoulders this morning when you think of *the needs of those among whom you live.* They are dying, perishing for lack of knowledge, rich and poor alike ignorant of Christ; multitudes of them wrapped up in self-righteousness. They are perishing, and those who ought to warn them are often dumb dogs that cannot bark. Do you not feel that you ought to deliver the sheep from the wolf? Have you no bowels of compassion? Are your hearts turned to steel? I am sure you cannot deny that the times demand of you earnest and forceful lives. No Christian man can now sit still without incurring awful guilt. Whether you live in London or in any other great town amidst reeking sin, or dwell in the country amidst the dense darkness which broods over many rural districts, you are under bonds to be up and doing. It may be a cross to you, but for Jesus' sake you must uplift it, and never lay it down till the Lord calls you home.

Some of you should bear the cross of Christ *because the cause of Christ is at discount where you dwell.* I delight in a man in whom the lordlier chivalry has found a congenial home. He loves to espouse the cause of truth in the cloudy and dark day. He never counts heads, but weighs arguments. When he settles down in a town he never inquires, "Where is the most respectable congregation? Where shall I meet with those who will advantage me in business?" No, he studies his conscience rather than his convenience. He hears one say, "There is a Nonconformist chapel, but it is down a back street. There is a Baptist church, but the members are nearly all poor, and no gentlefolk are among them. Even the evangelical church is down at the heel: the best families attend the high church." I say he hears this, and his heart is sick of such talk. He will go where the gospel is preached, and nowhere else. Fine architecture has scant charms for him, and grand music is no part of his religion : if these are substitutes for the gospel, he abhors them.

It is meanness itself for a man to forsake the truth for the sake of respectability. Multitudes who ought to be found maintaining the good old cause are recreant to their convictions, if indeed they ever had any. For this cause the true man resolves to stick to truth through thick and thin, and not to forsake her because her adherents are poor and despised. If ever we might temporize, that time is past and gone. I arrest yonder man this morning, who has long been a Christian, but has concealed half his Christianity in order to be thought respectable, or to escape the penalties of faithfulness. Come out from those with whom you are numbered, but with whom you are not united in heart. Be brave enough to defend a good cause against all comers; for the day shall come when he shall have honor for his guerdon who accepted dishonor that he might be true to his God, his Bible, and his conscience. Blessed be he who can be loyal to his Lord, cost him what it may—loyal even in those matters which traitors call little things. We would compel that Simon the Cyrenian this day to bear the cross, because there are so few to bear it in these degenerate days.

Besides, I may say to some of you, you ought to bear the cross because you know you are not satisfied; *your hearts are not at rest.* You have prospered in worldly things, but you are not happy; you have good health, but you are not happy; you have loving friends, but you are not happy. There is but one way of getting rest to the heart, and that is, to come to Jesus. That is His word: "Come unto me, ye that labor and are heavy laden, and I will give you rest." If after this you need a further rest for other and higher longings, then you must come again to the same Savior, and hearken to His next word: "Take my yoke upon you, and learn of me; for I am meek and lowly in heart: and ye shall find rest unto your souls. For my yoke is easy, and my burden is light." Some of you professors have not yet found perfect rest, and the reason is because you have looked to the cross for pardon, but you have never taken to cross-bearing as an occupation. You are hoping *in* Christ but not living *for* Christ. The finding of rest unto your soul will come to you in having something to do or to bear for Jesus. "Take my yoke upon you: and ye shall find rest unto your souls."

There are many ways, then, of bearing the cross for Christ, and there are many reasons why some here present should begin at once to the load.

Cross-bearing Is a Blessed Occupation

To close: bear with me a minute or two while I say that CROSS-BEARING IS A BLESSED OCCUPATION. I feel sure that Simon found it so. Let me mention certain blessings which must have attended the special service of Simon. First, *it brought him into Christ's company.* When they compelled him to bear His cross, he was brought close to Jesus. If it had not been for that compulsion, he might have gone his way, or might have been lost in the crowd; but now he is in the inner circle, near to Jesus. For the first time in his life he saw that blessed form, and as he saw it I believe his heart was enamored with it. As they lifted the cross on his shoulders he looked at that sacred Person, and saw a crown of thorns about His brow; and as he looked at his fellow-sufferer, he saw all down His cheeks the marks of bloody sweat, and black and blue bruises from cruel hands. As for those eyes, they looked him through and through! That face, that matchless face, he had never seen its like. Majesty was therein blended with misery, innocence with agony, and love with sorrow. He had never seen that countenance so well, nor marked the whole form of the Son of Man so clearly if he had not been called to bear that cross. It is wonderful how much we see of Jesus when we suffer or labor for Him. Believing souls, I pray that this day you may be so impressed into my Lord's service that you may have nearer and dearer fellowship with Him than in the past. If any man will do His will he shall know of the doctrine. They see Jesus best who carry His cross most.

Besides, *the cross held Simon in Christ's steps.* Do you catch it? If Jesus carried the front part of the cross and Simon followed behind, he was sure to put his feet down just where the Master's feet had been before. The cross is a wonderful implement for keeping us in the way of our Lord. As I was turning this subject over I was thinking how often I had felt a conscious contact between myself and my Lord when I have had to bear reproach for His sake; and how at the same time I have been led to watch my steps more carefully because of that very reproach. Beloved, we do not want to slip from under the cross. If we did so, we might slip away from our Lord and from holy walking. If we can keep our shoulder beneath that sacred load, and see our Lord a little on before, we shall be making the surest progress. This being near to Jesus is a blessed privilege, which is cheaply purchased at the price of cross-bearing. If you would see Jesus, bestir yourselves to work for Him. Boldly avow Him, cheerfully suffer for Him, and then you shall see Him, and then you shall learn to follow Him step by step. O blessed cross, which holds us to Jesus and to His ways!

Then Simon had this honor, that *he was linked with Christ's work.* He could not put away sin, but he could assist weakness. Simon did die on the cross to make expiation, but he did live under the cross to aid in the accomplishment of the divine purpose. You and I cannot interfere with Jesus in His passion, but we can share with Him in His compassion; we cannot purchase liberty for the enslaved, but we can tell them of their emancipation. To have a finger in Christ's work is glory. I invite the man who seeks honor and immortality, to seek it thus. To have a share in the Redeemer's work is a more attractive thing than all the pomp and glitter of this world, and the kingdoms thereof. Where are the men of heavenly mind who will covet to be joined unto the Lord in this ministry? Let them step out and say, "Jesus, I my cross have taken. Henceforth I will follow Thee. Come life or death, I will carry Thy cross till Thou shalt give me the crown."

While Simon was carrying the cross through the crowd, I doubt not that the rough soldiery would deal him many a kick or buffet; but I feel equally sure that the dear Master sometimes stole a glance at him. *Simon enjoyed Christ's smile.* I know the Lord so well, that I feel sure He must have done so: He would not forget the man who was His partner for the while. And O, that look! How Simon must have treasured up the remembrance of it. "I never carried a load that was so light," says he, "as that which I carried that morning; for when the Blessed One smiled at me amidst His woes, I felt myself to be strong as Hercules." Alexander, his first-born, and that red-headed lad Rufus, when they grew up both felt it to be the honor of the family that their father carried the cross after Jesus. Rufus and Alexander had a patent of nobility in being the sons of such a man.

Mark recorded the fact that Simon carried the cross, and that such and such persons were his sons. I think when the old man came to lie upon his deathbed he said: "My hope is in Him whose cross I carried. Blessed burden! Lay me down in my grave. This body of mine cannot perish, for it bore the cross which Jesus carried, and which carried *Him*. I shall rise again to see Him in His glory, for His cross has pressed me, and His love will surely raise me." Happy are we if we can while yet we live be coworkers together with Him, that when He comes in His kingdom we may be partakers of His glory. "Blessed is the man that endureth temptation: for when he is tried, he shall receive the crown of life, which the Lord hath promised to them that love him" God bless you, and especially you who have come out of the country. God bless you. Amen and amen.

10
*Unparalleled Suffering**

Christ also hath once suffered (1 Peter 3:18).

I t is very unpleasant to our poor flesh and blood to suffer. Physical pain is a grievous infliction; mental agony or spiritual sorrow is still worse. Irons around the wrists can be worn till they fit easily; but when the iron enters into the soul, how it rusts the heart, and eats into the spirit! Perhaps, to some minds, that is the hardest of all sufferings which is not deserved at all, but which comes because we do not deserve it; I mean, that suffering which innocent persons are called to endure because of their innocence, when they are slandered and oppressed and persecuted, not for evil-doing, but for well-doing. I admit that there is much about this form of trial which should tend to make it a light affliction, for we ought to take it joyfully when we suffer wrongfully. Yet, as a rule, we are not able to do so; certainly not by nature, for there is a sort of sense of justice within man which makes him feel that it is very hard that he should have to suffer, not for unrighteousness, but for righteousness; not for any wrong-doing, but for having espoused the cause of God and truth.

The apostle Peter would have Christians prepare themselves for this suffering. They had to bear very much of it in his day; they will have to bear some of it as long as ever the Church of Christ remains in this wicked world. He says, in the verse preceding our text: "It is better, if the will of God be so, that ye suffer for well-doing, than for evil-doing." Further on, at the beginning of the next chapter, he says: "Forasmuch then as Christ hath suffered for us in the flesh, arm yourselves likewise with the same mind." He warns us that we shall need to be clad in heavenly armor, for we shall have to pass through conflict and suffering for Christ's sake and for righteousness' sake. We must put on a coat of mail, and be enveloped in the whole panoply of God; we must have, as our great controlling principle,

---

* This sermon was intended for reading on Sunday, June 5, 1898, at the Metropolitan Tabernacle, Newington, and was preached on Sunday evening, March 4, 1883. It is taken from *The Metropolitan Tabernacle Pulpit.*

123

the mind of Christ, that, as He endured such contradiction of sinners against Himself, we also may endure it, and not be weary or faint in our minds. We shall best bear our own sufferings when we find fellowship with Christ in them. Hence, it is for your strengthening that your spiritual sinews may be braced, that you may be armed from head to foot, and preserved from the darts of the enemy, that I would set forth before you, as best I may, the matchless sufferings of the Son of God, who "once suffered for sins, the Just for the unjust, that He might bring us to God."

It has sometimes struck me that the first Epistle of Peter is greatly concerning Christ's first advent, and that his second Epistle tells us about our Lord's second advent. In this first letter, there are many references to the sufferings of Christ; it may interest you to notice some of them. In the first chapter, at the eleventh verse, we read: "Searching what, or what manner of time the Spirit of Christ which was in them did signify, when it testified beforehand the sufferings of Christ." When the apostle gets to the second chapter, at the twenty-first verse, we find him writing thus: "For even hereunto were ye called: because Christ also suffered for us, leaving us an example, that ye should follow his steps." Next comes our text in the third chapter; then, in the fourth chapter, at the first verse, is the passage I have already read to you; and in the thirteenth verse, the apostle says: "Rejoice, inasmuch as ye are partakers of Christ's sufferings"; and in the fifth chapter, at the first verse, he calls himself "a witness of the sufferings of Christ." Thus his frequent expression—his peculiar idiom—is, "the sufferings of Christ"; and in the language of our text he thus describes the great work of our redemption: "Christ also hath once suffered." It may seem a very small thing to you to call your attention to such words as these, but it does not appear small to me. It seems to me that there is a great depth of meaning within these few words, and it shall be my object, at this time, to bring out that meaning, as far as I can, under the Holy Spirit's guidance.

A Summary without Any Details

Notice then, first of all, A SUMMARY WITHOUT ANY DETAILS. "Christ also hath once suffered." There is compassed within that expression a summary of the whole life and death of Christ. The apostle does not give us details of Christ's sufferings; but he lets us, for a moment, look into this condensation of them: "Christ also hath once suffered."

It is *the epitome of His whole earthly existence* up to the time of His rising from the dead. Christ begins His life here with suffering. He is born into the world, but there is "no room for him in the inn." He must be in a manger, where the horned oxen feed. He is born of a poor mother, He must know the ills of poverty; and, worse still, Herod seeks the young Child's life. He must be hurried away by night into Egypt; He must be a stranger in a strange land, with His life in peril from a bloodthirsty tyrant. When He comes back from Egypt, He grows in wisdom and stature, and in favor with God and men; but you may rest assured that the years He spent in the carpenter's shop at Nazareth, though we are not told about them, were years of sore travail—perhaps, of bodily pain; certainly, of mental toil and preparation for His future service. Such a public life as His could not have been lived without due training. I will not attempt to lift the veil where God has let it fall; but I see, in the whole public ministry of Christ, traces of a wonderful mental discipline through which he must have gone, and which, I should think, must have involved Him in suffering. Certainly, it was one main point in His preparation that He was not without spiritual conflicts and struggles, which must have involved suffering to such a nature as His was.

No sooner does He appear on the stage of action, and the Spirit of God descends upon Him in the waters of baptism, than He is hurried off to a forty days' fast in the wilderness, and to a prolonged and terrible conflict with His great enemy and ours. Of that time, we may truly say that "*he suffered, being tempted.*" Throughout His life, you may read such words as these: "Jesus, being weary, sat thus on the well"; "Foxes have holes, and the birds of the air have nests, but the Son of man hath not where to lay his head"; and then you can understand some of the ways in which He suffered. We cannot tell how much our Lord suffered even in the brightest portion of His career, for always was He "despised and rejected of men; a man of sorrows, and acquainted with grief." We cannot go into all the details of His life; but I think you may see that, even in the very smoothest part of it, He suffered, and Peter does well thus to sum it up: "Christ suffered."

But when He comes to *Gethsemane*, shall I speak of the bloody sweat and the groans which startled angels? No, I need not say more than this: "Christ suffered." Shall I tell of His betrayal by Judas, of His being hurried from bar to bar, falsely accused, despitefully entreated, bruised, and scourged, and made nothing of? Truly, I may sum it all up by saying that He suffered. And as for all the rest, that march along the *Via Dolorosa*— that fastening to the wood—that uplifting of the cross, the wounds, the cruel fever, the direful thirst, the mockery, the scorn, the desertion of His Father when He must at last yield Himself up to death itself—what better summary could even an inspired apostle give than to say, "Christ also hath once suffered"? This expression sums up the whole of His life.

It is well for you and for me, when we have the time and the opportunity, to make as complete as possible our knowledge of Christ as to all the details of His life and death; but, just now, it must suffice us, as it sufficed Peter, to say, "Christ suffered." When next you are called to suffer, when pains of body oppress you, let this text whisper in your ear, "Christ also hath, once suffered." When you are poor, and needy, and homeless, recollect that "Christ also hath once suffered"; and when you come even to the agony of death, if such shall be your portion, then still hear the soft whisper, "Christ hath once suffered." I know of no better armor for you than this: "Arm yourselves likewise with the same mind"; and be prepared to count it your honor and glory to follow your Master with the cross upon your shoulders.

Much may be said to be known concerning Christ's sufferings; but, still, to a great extent, they are unknown sufferings. Some eyes saw Him suffer, yet I might truly say, "Eye hath not seen, neither hath ear heard, neither hath entered into the heart of man the things which Christ suffered for his people." You may think, brethren, that you know something of Christ's sufferings; but they are a deep unfathomable, a height to which the human imagination cannot soar. We are obliged to leave this summary without any details: "Christ also hath once suffered."

> Much we talk of Jesus' blood,
> But, how little's understood!
> Of His sufferings, so intense,
> Angels have no perfect sense.
>
> Who can rightly comprehend
> Their beginning or their end?
> Tis to God and God alone
> That their weight is fully known.

A Statement without Any Limit

Secondly, this is A STATEMENT WITHOUT ANY LIMIT. How indefinitely it is put! "Christ also hath once suffered."

Do you ask the question, *"When did Christ suffer?"* It is answered by not being answered; for, truly, we may reply to you—When Christ was on earth, when was there that He did not suffer? "Christ also hath once suffered." The apostle adds no note of time; he says not, "Christ suffered on the cross," or, "in the garden"; but the very indefiniteness of the statement leaves us to understand that, as long as Jesus was here, He was the acquaintance of grief. His life was, in a sense, a life of suffering. All the while He was here, even when He was not upon the cross, and even when no bloody sweat was on His brow, it is written, "Himself took our infirmities, and bare our sicknesses." He was bearing the load, not as some say, "on the tree" alone, but *up to the tree*, as the passage may be read—daily bearing it till, at length, He came to the cross, and there it was for the last time that He felt the pressure of human sin. You cannot get, and yet you do in some sense get, from my text, an answer to the question, "When did Christ suffer?"

Perhaps another asks, *"What did Christ suffer?"* The text is remarkable in giving here no limit whatever to the statement: "Christ also hath once suffered." What did He suffer? I answer—What was there that He did not suffer in body, in mind, and in spirit? What of pain—what of shame—what of loss—what of hatred—what of derision? He suffered from hell, from earth, from heaven—I was going to say—from time and from eternity; for there was a certain sense in which eternal pangs passed through the heart of Christ, and spent themselves upon Him. What did He suffer? Peter says, as if that should be enough for us to know, "Christ hath once suffered"— the very indefiniteness implies that He suffered everything that He could suffer.

And *where did Christ suffer*? Peter does not answer that question. Where did He suffer? In the wilderness? In the garden? In Pilate's hall? On the cross? The text as good as says, "Nay; yea; not somewhere only, but everywhere." Wherever He was, still was Christ enduring that great burden which He came into the world to bear till He should carry it away, and it should be lost forever.

From whom did Christ suffer? Mark how unlimited is the text: "Christ also hath once suffered." From men falsely accusing Him, and slandering Him? Yes; and that is the comfort of His slandered people; but He suffered not from wicked men alone, but even from good men; the best of His disciples cost Him many pangs, and sometimes made His heart ache. He suffered from devils. He suffered from the Father Himself. There it stands—a sky without horizon—a sea across which I look, and see no end or bound: "Christ also hath once suffered." I think that Joseph Hart spoke well when he said that Christ—

> Bore all incarnate God could bear,
> With strength enough, and none to spare.

So we leave this part of our theme; it is a statement without any limit: "Christ also hath once suffered."

A Description without Any Addition

Now I want you to notice, in the third place, that this is A DESCRIPTION WITHOUT ANY ADDITION.

> "Christ also hath once suffered."

Is that all? Was there not something else? No; this line sweeps the entire circumference. There was nothing in Christ, before His suffering, which was contrary to it. He never regretted that He had entered upon a course which involved suffering. "When the time was come that he should be received up, he stedfastly set his face to go to Jerusalem," warning His followers that He was going there to be mocked, and to be scourged, and to be crucified. He might, at any moment, have relinquished His terrible task, but that idea never entered into His mind. Even when He came near to the worst part of His pain, and His human nature shrank from it, His true heart never was discouraged, or thought of turning back. He said, "The cup which my Father hath given me, shall I not drink it?" And He did drink it, though it involved more suffering than we can imagine; yet there was no resistance to that suffering.

He suffered, but He never rebelled against it; He could truly say, "I was not rebellious, neither turned away back." He did not even complain, and Isaiah's prophecy was literally fulfilled by Him: "He is brought as a lamb to the slaughter, and as a sheep before her shearers is dumb, so he openeth not his mouth." If we were to describe the experiences of even the best of men, I am afraid that we should have to say, "He suffered very much, but he did not often murmur. Sometimes, however, he rebelled, and cried out." It was not so with Christ. Peter says, He suffered; and there is no addition to that. You know, my brethren, how, having undertaken to suffer for sins, He went through with it. If He stood before Pilate, and His enemies smote Him, what did He do? He suffered. If they bound His eyes, and buffeted Him, what did He do? He suffered. When they spat into His face, what did He do? He suffered. When they nailed Him to the cross, what words did He speak against His murderers? Not one; He suffered: "Who, when he was reviled, reviled not again.'' Even when they jested at Him, His only reply was the prayer, "Father, forgive them; for they know not what they do."

He suffered; and there was nothing to take away from the completeness of that suffering. The whole of His nature ran out into that act of obedience called suffering; it was the time when He must do the Father's will by suffering, and all the power of His being ran into that channel. The Lord had made to meet upon Him the iniquity, and, consequently, the suffering, of us all; and He just accepted it at the Father's hand without a complaint or a murmur. You can sum it all up in the language of our text, without a single word added to it: "Christ also hath once suffered."

A Declaration without Any Qualifications

Once more, I want you to notice that this is A DECLARATION WITHOUT ANY QUALIFICATIONS.

"Christ suffered."

There is no word to bid us imagine that He had *any alleviation of His agony.* Of a person in very bad health we may be able to say, "He suffers a great deal; but he has an excellent medical attendant, and a good nurse, and he has every comfort that can be given to him." But, in the case of our Lord, all is summed up in these two words, "Christ suffered." Were there no comforters? No; He suffered. Was there no sleeping-draught to deaden His pain? No; He suffered. But did not His Father help Him in the hour of His agony? No; His cry, "My God, my God, why hast thou forsaken me?" proves that we may say of Him, even with reference to God, that He suffered.

The death of Christ was quite unique; none of the martyrs were ever brought into the same condition as their Lord was in. I remember reading in Foxe's *Book of Martyrs* the story of a man of God, who was bound to a stake to die for Christ; there he was, calm and quiet, till his legs had been burned away, and the bystanders looked to see his helpless body drop from the chains. He was black as coal, and not a feature could be discerned; but one who was near was greatly surprised to see that poor black carcass open its mouth, and two words came out of it; and what do you suppose they were? "Sweet Jesus!" And then the martyr fell over the chains, and at last life was gone. O, how much of the blessed presence of God that poor saint must have had to be able to say, at the last, when he was charred to a coal, "Sweet Jesus!"

But the Lord Jesus had not that help and comfort. His Father's countenance was hidden from Him. "Eloi, Eloi, lama sabachthani," is such a shriek as even hell itself has never heard, for the lost ones there have never known what it was to have the love of God shed abroad in their hearts, as Christ had known it; and, therefore, they could never know the loss of it as Christ knew it in that supreme moment of His agony. "Christ suffered." That is all you can say of Him, He suffered, without any alleviation of His pain.

Further, He suffered *without any qualification, in the sense of being compelled to suffer.* We say of such-and-such a person, "He suffers greatly, but he cannot help suffering; he has a deadly disease, the pain of which cannot be alleviated; he is, therefore, obliged to bear it." The martyr, whom I mentioned just now, was bound to the stake; he could not get away, he suffered under compulsion, he was made to suffer. But you cannot say that of Christ. Herein is a marvelous thing that, while Christ suffered, you may take the word in the active sense. I do not know how exactly to express my meaning, but there is a sort of passive sense in which He suffered, and that is the sense in which we all suffer according to our share; but Jesus also suffered in an active sense; that is to say, He suffered willingly; resolutely, without any compulsion. At any moment, He might have broken loose from the cross, He might have called for twelve legions of angels, and scattered all His foes; He might have flung off His body, and appeared before them as a consuming fire utterly to destroy them; or, retaining His humanity, He might have smitten them with blindness, or wrought some other miracle, and so have escaped from them.

If we should be called to die for Christ, it would only be paying the debt of nature a little beforehand, for we are bound to die sooner or later; it is the lot of man. But there was no such need in the case of Christ; there was no necessity of death about that holy thing which was born of the Virgin Mary. It would not corrupt, and it needed not to die. All the way through His death, remember that He did not die as we do—gradually losing consciousness, floating away, and never able to suspend the process of dissolution; but, at any instant, up to the final committal of His spirit to His Father, He could have caused all those pains to cease. Now see with what an extraordinary meaning my text is girt about. As the painters foolishly depict Christ with a halo round His head which was never there, I may truly picture His sufferings, mystically and spiritually, with a halo about them which is really there, for He suffered, in this superhuman fashion, without any qualification as to alleviation or as to compulsion.

Dear friends, how shall I speak further upon this part of my subject? Only this word would I add—that Christ suffered *without any desert.* If we suffer, we must say to ourselves that we suffer less than we deserve; and even when a man suffers so as to die, we know that death is the penalty of sin. But "Christ suffered" in a very special sense because "in him was no sin." He had never done anything worthy of death, or of bonds. He suffered "for sins not his own." There was nothing about Him that brought the suffering upon Him; His was the suffering of a pure and holy Being. We say of a criminal, not so much that he suffers, but that he is punished, he is executed, he is put to death.

We never say that of Christ. We say that He suffered. Voluntarily, and without any obligation on account of demerit, He comes and takes upon Himself the sins of His people, stands in their stead, is chastened with their chastisements, is smitten with their smiting. Well does He say, by the mouth of the psalmist, "Many a time have they afflicted me from my youth: yet they have not prevailed against me. The ploughers ploughed upon my back: they made long their furrows." So indeed they did, not only on His back, but on His heart. I am speaking now, not only of His external but of His internal sufferings. Truly did one say that "the sufferings of Christ's soul were the very soul of His sufferings"; and so, no doubt, they were; but, in His case, there was no punishment due to Him, so in His sufferings there was nothing exacted from Him on His own account. I must leave you to think upon this great mystery, for I cannot speak of it as it deserves.

An Expression with an Emphasis:
"Christ also hath once suffered."

I close with this last reflection. My text is AN EXPRESSION WITH AN EMPHASIS: "CHRIST ALSO HATH ONCE SUFFERED." When we think of our own sufferings, as compared with our Lord's, we may print them in the smallest type that the printer can use; but where shall I find capital letters that are large enough to print this sentence when it applies to Him—

"CHRIST ALSO HATH ONCE SUFFERED"? It is almost as if the apostle said, "You have none of you suffered when compared with Him"; or, at least, He was the Arch-Sufferer—the Prince of sufferers—the Emperor of the realm of agony—Lord paramount in sorrow.

Just take that term, "a man of sorrows." You know that, in the Book of Revelation, there is the expression, "the man of sin." What does "the man of sin" mean but a man made up of sin, one who is all sin? Very well, then, "a man of sorrows" means a man made up of sorrows, constructed of sorrows—sorrows from the crown of His head to the sole of His foot—sorrow without and sorrow within. He did sleep with sorrow, and wake with sorrow; He was a man of sorrow, a mass of sorrow. Take the next expression, "and acquainted with grief." Grief was His familiar acquaintance, not a person that He passed by, and casually addressed, but His acquaintance that kept close to Him throughout His life. He said once, "Lover and friend hast thou put far from me, and mine acquaintance into darkness"; but this acquaintance was with Him there: "acquainted with grief."

Listen to the words; and if you can see my Lord, pressed by the strong arm of grief until He is covered all over with a gory shirt of bloody sweat, then you know that grief had made Him to be acquainted with its desperate tugs. When you see Him bleeding at His hands, and feet, and side, with all His spirit exceeding sorrowful even unto death, and God Himself leaving Him in the thick darkness, then you know that He was indeed acquainted with grief.

You know a little about grief, but you do not know much. The hem of grief's garment is all you ever touch, but Christ wore it as His daily robe. We do but sip of the cup; He drank it to its bitterest dregs. We feel just a little of the warmth of Nebuchadnezzar's furnace; but He dwelt in the very midst of the fire.

There I must leave the whole matter with you; but, as you come to the communion table, come with this one thought upon you: "Christ also hath once suffered." Somebody perhaps asks me, "Is there any comfort in that thought?" Is it not a wonderful thing that there should be more of comfort in the sufferings of Christ than in any other thing under heaven? Yet it is so; there is more joy in the sufferings of Christ, to those whose hearts are broken, or sorely wounded, than there is in His birth, or His resurrection, or anything else about the Savior. It is by His stripes rather than even by His glory we are healed. Come, beloved, take a draught from this bitter wine, which shall sweetly charm away all your sorrows, and make you glad. May God, the Holy Spirit, grant that it may be so! And if there is anybody here who is not saved, remember, friend, that your salvation depends upon the sufferings of Christ. If you believe on Him, then His sufferings are yours, they have taken away your sin, and you are clear. Therefore, go your way, and be glad.

11

Christ's Connection with Sinners the Source of His Glory*

Therefore will I divide Him a portion with the great, and he shall divide the spoil with the strong; because he hath poured out his soul unto death: and he was numbered with the transgressors; and he bare the sin of many, and made intercession for the transgressors (Isaiah 53:12).

We may regard this verse as a kind of covenant made between the everlasting God, the infinite Jehovah, on the one part, and our great Representative, Mediator, and Redeemer, the Lord Jesus Christ, on the other. The incarnate God is to be bruised and wounded; He is to pour out His soul unto death, and by a travail of soul He is to bear the sin of many; and then His ultimate reward is to be, that God will divide Him a portion with the great, and He Himself shall divide the spoil with the strong. Note the double recompense, and joyfully distinguish between the two divisions—that which Jehovah makes for Him, and that which He makes Himself. Our champion, like another David, is to confront and conquer the great enemy of the Lord's people, and then He is to have His reward. Unlike David, He is to pour out His soul, and die in the conflict, and then He is to receive a glorious portion from the Father, and He is also Himself to seize upon the spoil of the vanquished foe.

At this moment, our Lord Jesus is enjoying the reward which His Father has allotted Him: "Therefore will I divide him a portion with the great." He is no more despised and rejected. Who dare do dishonor to a majesty so surpassing? See how the whole host of heaven adores Him! All the pomp of glory is displayed around Him. To Him the cherubim and seraphim con-

---

* This sermon was intended for reading on Sunday, February 17, 1889, at the Metropolitan Tabernacle, Newington. It is taken from *The Metropolitan Tabernacle Pulpit.*

132

tinually do cry, in their ceaseless worship and undivided adoration. The four-and-twenty elders, representing the ancient and the present church, cast crowns at His feet; and the myriads of the redeemed, whose robes are washed in His blood, pour forth their love, and life, at His feet. He has His portion with the great; none are so great as He. He is not only King, but king-maker, for He has made His humblest followers priests and kings unto God, and His royalty is multiplied in each of them. How much His Father honors Him, it is not for my tongue to tell you; and, if it were possible for me to tell it in words, yet the inner meaning could never be compassed by such narrow hearts as ours. He has infinite glory from the great Father God. He lives forever, King of kings and Lord of lords, and all hallelujahs come up before Him. Imagination cannot reach the height of His immeasurable majesty and felicity.

And why these honors? What has He done to merit these immeasurable glories? The answer is that He has done these four things: "he hath poured out his soul unto death: and he was numbered with the transgressors; and he bare the sin of many, and made intercession for the transgressors."

In addition to what his Father gives Him, it is worthy of contemplation that our Lord has taken, in His life-conflict, great spoils with His own hands. "He shall divide the spoil with the strong." He has spoiled sin, death, and hell; each one the vanquisher of our race, the spoiler of the entire world. He has overcome these three, and in each case has led captivity captive. What must be the spoils of such victories? All the processions of triumph that ever went up the Sacra Via to the Capitol of Rome we may dismiss as empty pageants; all the glories of Assyria, Babylon, Persia, and Greece, are blots of the cruel past, which sicken us in remembrance. These led liberty captive; but when He ascended on high, He led *captivity* captive. Jesus blesses all by His victories, and curses none. He spoiled no man of His goods: He only brought death on death, destruction on the destroyer, and captivity upon captivity. In all His spoils men are gainers; and, therefore, when the incarnate God divides the spoil with the strong, all His people may joyfully shout without the reservation of a sigh for the conquered and the spoiled. That was a rich triumph, and the spoils He won are spoils that enrich myriads of believers today, and shall enrich them throughout all the ages that are to come.

And why these spoils? What has He done? These trophies—where were they won? What was the conflict? Here is the answer: "Because he hath poured out his soul unto death: and he was numbered with the transgressors; and he bare the sin of many, and made intercession for the transgressors."

It is a strange fact that I am going to declare, but it is not less true than strange: *according to our text the extraordinary glories of Christ, as Savior, have all been earned by His connection with human sin*. He has gotten His most illustrious splendor, His brightest jewels, His divinest crowns, out of coming into contact with this poor fallen race. What is man? What are all men? Nothings, nobodies. This great globe itself—what is it in connection with the vast creation of God? One grain of the sweepings of dust behind the door. The small dust of the balance bears a larger proportion to the eternal hills than this little globe to the great worlds which speak to us across the midnight sky. Yet all those glittering worlds that we can see with the telescope bear an extremely minute proportion to the illimitable fields of divine creation. Yet, we know not that anywhere Christ ever came into contact with sin, except upon this little ball. We have no revelation of any other redemption. This obscure star is faith's great marvel!

How shall we comprehend that here the eternal Deity did take the nature of a man, and here did suffer in the sinner's stead "the just for the unjust, that he might bring us to God"? All the eyes of all the angels turn this way. This mystery is too great for them. They cannot compass its full meaning, but desire to look into it. We know not, that anywhere in all the vast creation of God, there has ever been seen the like of this matchless, unparalleled deed of grace—that the Son of God, in mighty love, should come down to earth, and come into contact with human sin, that He might put it away. No one imagines that our Lord has often suffered. No, He has been incarnate once, and has been sacrificed but once. "Once in the end of the world hath he appeared to put away sin by the sacrifice of himself." And this for guilty men! I am overwhelmed. I would fain sit down in silence, and give way to adoring wonder.

May the Holy Spirit Himself now aid me, for my need is great! I am going to speak about these four things, very briefly. I have nothing of my own to say about them. I only want to put them before you as much as I can in their naked simplicity: there is a beauty in them which needs no describing, which would be degraded by any adornment of human speech. Here are four flints out of which you may strike sparks of divine fire, if you are but willing to see their brightness. These four things that Jesus did, the four reasons why He is crowned with such superlative honor, are connected with you, if you have but faith to perceive the connection— so connected that they will save you, will even make you partake in the glory which has come of them.

He Has Poured Out His Soul unto Death

The first source of the Mediator's glory is, that, out of His love to guilty men, HE HAS POURED OUT HIS SOUL UNTO DEATH. Remember that the penalty of sin is death. "The soul that sinneth, it shall die." "For in the day that thou eatest thereof thou shalt surely die." As God made us we should not have died. There is about man when he is in connection with God no reason or room for death; but as soon as man touched evil, he was divided from God, and he took into his veins the poison which brings death with it, and all its train of woes. Jesus Christ, our substitute, when He poured out His soul unto death, was bearing the penalty that is due to sin. This is taught in the Bible: in fact, it is the chief theme of Holy Scripture.

Whenever sin was to be put away, it was by the sacrifice of a life. All through the Jewish law it stands conspicuous that, "Without shedding of blood is no remission of sin." God has so impressed this truth upon humanity that you can scarcely go into any nation, however benighted, but there is connected with their religion the idea of sacrifice, and therefore the idea of the offering of a life on account of a broken law. Now, the Lord Jesus came into such connection with men that He bore the death penalty which guilty men had incurred.

Notice the expression: "he hath poured out his soul unto death." *It is deliberate.* "He hath poured out his soul." It is a libation presented with thought and care; not the mere spilling of His blood, but the resolute, determinate pouring out of His whole life unto its last drop—the pouring it out unto death. Now, Christ's resolve to die for you and for me was not that of a brave soldier, who rushes up to the cannon's mouth in a moment of excitement; but He was practically pouring out His life from the day when His public ministry commenced, if not before. He was always dying by living at such a rate that his zeal consumed Him—"The zeal of thine house hath eaten me up." Deliberately, and as it were drop by drop, He was letting His soul fall upon the ground, till at length, upon the tree of doom, He emptied it all out, and cried, "It is finished," and gave up the ghost. Then "he poured out his soul unto death."

As it was deliberate, so *it was most real and true.* I pray you do not think of Christ as pouring out His soul, as though the outpouring was a kind of sentiment of self-abnegation; as though it made Him spend a sort of ecstatic life in dream-land, and suffer only in thought, intent, and sympathy. My Lord suffered as you suffer, only more keenly; for He had never injured His body or soul by any act of excess, so as to take off the edge from His sensitiveness. His was the pouring out of a whole soul in all the phases of suffering into which perfect souls can pass. He felt the horror of sin as we who have sinned could not feel it, and the sight of evil afflicted Him much more than it does the purest among us.

His was real suffering, real poverty, real weariness; and when He came to His last agony, His bloody sweat was no fiction, His exceeding sorrow unto death was no fancy. When the scourges fell upon His shoulders it was true pain that He suffered; and the nails, and the spear, and the sponge, and the vinegar—these tell of a real passion—a death such as probably you and I shall never know. Certainly we shall never experience that pouring out of His soul unto death which was peculiar to Jesus, in which He went far beyond martyrs in their extremest griefs. There were points of anguish about His death which were for Himself, and for Himself alone. "He hath poured out his soul unto death," in grief most weighty—so weighty that it can never be fully weighed in any scales of mortal sympathy.

And He did this, remember, voluntarily. If I were to die for any one of you, what would it amount to but that I paid the debt of nature a little sooner than I must ultimately have paid it? For we must all die, sooner or later. But the Christ needed not to die at all, so far as He Himself was personally concerned. There was no cause within Himself why He should go to the cross to lay down His life. He yielded Himself up, a willing sacrifice for our sins. Herein lies much of the preciousness of His propitiation to you and to me. Love, love immeasurable, led the immortal Lord to die for man. Let us think it over, and melt into loving gratitude. A death endured out of pure love; a death which was altogether unnecessary on His own account, and indeed a superfluous act, save that it behooved Him to suffer that He might fulfill His office of a Savior, and bring us near to God; this is a matter which should set our heart on fire with fervent gratitude to the Lord who loved us to the death.

"He hath poured out his soul unto death." I will say no more about it, except that you see *how complete* it was. Jesus gave poor sinners everything. His every faculty was laid out for them. To His last rag He was stripped upon the cross. No part of His body or of His soul was kept back from being made a sacrifice. The last drop, as I said before, was poured out till the cup was drained. He made no reserve: He kept not back even His innermost self: "He hath poured out his soul unto death."

Consider these two truths together. He is the Lord God Almighty, before whom the hosts of angels bow with joy; yet on yonder cross He pours out His soul unto death; and He does it, not because of anything that is in Him that renders it needful, but for your sakes, and for mine—for the salvation of all those who put their trust in Him. Put your trust in Him, then, without reserve. Pour out your souls in full trust, even as He poured out His soul unto death. Come, and rest in Him, and then see the reason why He is crowned with majesty. His death for your sins is the reason why He divides the spoils with the strong. He has His portion with the great because He "died, the just for the unjust, that he might bring us to God." This, which brought Him so much shame, has now brought Him all His glory. Come, and trust Him! Come, and trust Him wholly! Come, and trust Him now!

He was Numbered with Sinners

Secondly, and somewhat briefly. It appears in the text, that our Lord did not only bear the penalty due to sinners, but HE WAS NUMBERED WITH SINNERS. "He was numbered with the transgressors." There is a touch of nearness to the sinner about this which there is not in the first clause. He bears death for the sinner; but you could not suppose, if you had not read it, that He would be written in the sinners' register. He was not, and could not, be a sinner; but yet it is written, "He was numbered with the transgressors." O sinner, see how close Jesus comes to you! Is there a census taken of sinners? Then, in that census, the name of Jesus is written down. "He was numbered with the transgressors." He never was a transgressor: it was impossible that He could be.

It would be blasphemy to say that the Son of God ever was a transgressor against His Father's laws. In Him was no sin in any sense, or shape, or manner. His spotless birth, His perfect nature, His holy life, all make Him "separate from sinners." How, then, was He numbered with the transgressors? This makes it the more marvelous, because it is so hurtful to a man who is pure, to be numbered with the impure. What would any woman with a delicate purity of mind think, if she were numbered with the harlots? What would any honest man among us think if he were numbered with thieves? But that would be nothing compared with the holy Lord Jesus being numbered with the transgressors; and yet to this He submitted for our sakes. I said that He could not be a transgressor; but we are not like Him in this. Any one of us could be either unjust or dishonest; for, alas! sin dwells in us, and the possibilities of its still greater development; but Jesus was clean in nature, and pure in heart, and therefore He could never be tainted with evil; and yet the inspired prophet says, "He was numbered with the transgressors." This was a stoop, indeed! This was coming down to where the sinner lay, and bowing over Him to lift Him up.

Our Lord Jesus was numbered with the transgressors, first, *by the tongue of slander.* They called Him a drunken man and a wine-bibber: they even called Him Beelzebub. That was sharp enough for Him to bear, whom all the angels salute as "Holy, holy, holy!" Accused of blasphemy, sedition, and so forth, He had enough to bear from evil lips. Nothing was too vile to be cast upon Him by those who said, "Let him be crucified." Reproach never spared the spotless one; but spent its utmost venom on Him. Like the Psalmist, He was the song of the drunkard. The very thieves who were crucified with Him reviled Him.

He was numbered with the transgressors *in the earthly courts of justice.* He stood at the bar as a common felon, though He was judge of all. Though they could not find witnesses, whose testimony agreed, yet they condemned Him. Though Pilate had to say, "Why, what evil hath he done?" yet He was taken out with two malefactors, that He might die side by side with them; and then, we are told by the evangelist, the Scripture was fulfilled—"He was numbered with the transgressors" (Mark 15:28).

To go a little farther, our Lord Jesus Christ, on earth, *was treated, in the providence of God, as transgressors are treated.* Transgression sometimes brings on men poverty, sickness, reproach, and desertion; and Jesus Christ had to take His share of all these with sinful men. No wind was tempered for this shorn lamb. No winter's frost was stayed, no night dews dried to comfort His secret agonies.

> Cold mountains and the midnight air
> Witnessed the fervor of His prayer.

All things in this world that are so keen and terrible to man, because man has become so guilty, were just as keen and terrible to Him. The sun shone on Him till His tongue was dried up like a potsherd, and did cleave to His jaws, and He cried, "I thirst." The nails that pierced Him tore His tender flesh as they would have torn that of the sinful. Fever parched Him till His tongue cleaved to His jaws. There was no softening of the laws of nature for this Man, because He had never offended; but He had to stand as a sinner where we sinners stand, to suffer from the common laws of a sin-cursed world, though He was not and could not be a sinner. "In him was no sin"; yet He was numbered with the transgressors.

And look, my brethren. O that I may know how to speak properly on it! The Holy God treated Him as if He were one of us: "it pleased the Father to bruise him; he hath put him to grief." God not only turned His back on transgressors, but He turned His back upon His Son, who was numbered with them. God never can forsake the perfectly innocent, yet He who was perfectly innocent said, "My God, my God, why hast thou forsaken me?" Sinking and anguish of spirit, even to soul-death, cannot come to a man who is numbered with the perfectly righteous. It was because Jesus voluntarily put Himself into the sinner's place that He had to bear the sinner's doom; and, He being numbered with the transgressors, the justice which smites sin smote Him, the frown that falls on sin fell on Him, the darkness which comes over human sin gathered in sevenfold night about His sacred brow. In the day of the Lord's anger, "He was numbered with the transgressors."

As this is the reason why He is now exalted, it seems to me that you and I ought to feel a mingling of grief and joy at this time to think that the Lord Jesus would condescend to put His name down with transgressors. You know what a transgressor is, do you not? One who has done wrong; one who has broken laws; one who has gone beyond bounds and committed evil. Well, Jesus Christ says, "Father, that I might save these transgressors, put my name down among them." It was necessary that it should be so, that He, standing in their stead, might lift them into His place, transferring His righteousness to them, as He took their sin upon Himself. I could weep as I tell you that "He was numbered with the transgressors." I cannot preach. This theme baffles me altogether. I wish that you would look into it yourselves. Never mind my words. Think of my Lord, and of these two things: "He hath poured out his soul unto death: and he was numbered with the transgressors."

He Bare the Sin of Many

That leads me to the third matter by which the Lord Jesus Christ has won His victories, and earned reward of God. It is this: HE BARE THE SIN OF MANY. Now, do not think that these words are mine, and therefore cavil at them. Deliberately observe that these are the words of the Holy Spirit. "He bare the sin": "He bare the sin of many." They cavil at us for saying that He bare the chastisement of sin. We shall say it none the less plainly; but we shall go much further, and insist upon it that, literally, Jesus bare the sin of man. Else, why did He die? Why did He die at all? "He was man," say you, "and, therefore, He died." There was no reason why the Christ should die because He was a man, for, being born without the taint of sin, and having lived a spotless life, and having never violated the law of God, there could be no justice in Christ's dying at all, if there was not some reason for it apart from Himself.

It is an act of injustice that Jesus should be permitted to die at all, unless there can be found a reason apart from His own personal conduct. If death be the consequence of sin, there being no sin in Christ, the consequence could not follow without the cause. You tell me that by wicked hands He was crucified: it was so, and yet the Scripture assures us that this was by the determinate purpose and foreknowledge of God. How could this have been had our Lord no connection with sin? It was not of necessity that He should die because He was man. He might have been taken to heaven in a chariot of fire; or it might have been said of Him, as of Enoch, "He was not, for God took him." If the rough Elias ascended to heaven, how much more the gentle, tender, perfect, absolutely perfect, Christ, might have been expected to do so! There was no reason, then, in His personal nature, why He should die.

"He died," said one, "as an example." But, my dear friends, I do not see that. In His life He is an example to us through and through, and so He is in His death. If we must needs die, it is an example to us that we should die as bravely, as patiently, as believingly as He did; but we are not bound to die at all unless God requires it at our hands. Indeed, we are bound to shun death if it can virtuously be avoided. Self-preservation is a law of nature; and for any man to voluntarily give of himself up to die without some grand purpose would not be justifiable. It is only because there is a law that we must die that we may judge ourselves permitted to volunteer to die. The Savior does not set us an example in a sphere into which we cannot enter. In that case He goes beyond us altogether, and treads the wine-press alone. He is a Being whom we cannot follow in the higher walks in which He is both God and man. In His great voluntary self-surrender unto death, the Son of God stoops from a position which we, who are mortal because of sin, have never held.

"Well," say you, "but Jesus Christ died as an exhibition of divine love." This is true in a certain sense, but from another point of view, of all the things I have ever heard, this does seem to me to be the most monstrous statement that could be made. That Jesus Christ, dying because of our sins, is a wonderful example of divine love, I do know, admit, and glory in; but that Christ's dying was an instance of divine love, if He did not die because He bare our sins, I entirely deny. There is no exhibition of divine love in the death of Christ if it be not for our sins, but an exhibition of a very different sort.

The death of the perfect Son of God, *per se*, and without its great object, does not exhibit love, but the reverse. What? Does God put to death His only begotten Son, the perfectly pure and holy being? Is this the *finale* of a life of obedience? Well, then, I see no love in God at all. It seems to me to be the reverse of love that it should be so.

Apart from sin-bearing, the statement that Jesus must needs die the death of the cross to show us that His Father is full of love is sheer nonsense; but if He died in our room and stead, then the gift of Jesus Christ by the Father is undoubtedly a glorious instance of divine love. Behold, and wonder, that "God so loved the world, that he gave his only begotten Son, that whosoever believeth in him should not perish, but have everlasting life." This is love, if you please; but not the mere fact that the Son of God should be put to death. That were a thing altogether unaccountable, not to be justified, but to be looked upon as a horrible mystery never to be explained—that the blessed Son of God should die—if we did not receive this full and complete explanation, "He bare the sin of many."

If our Lord's bearing our sin for us is not the gospel, I have no gospel to preach. Brethren, I have befooled you these five-and-thirty years, if this is not the gospel. I am a lost man, if this is not the gospel; for I have no hope beneath the copes of heaven, neither in time nor in eternity, save only in this belief, that Jesus, in my stead, bore both my punishment and sin.

If our Lord did so bear our sin we have a firm and joyous confidence. God would not accept a substitute in our place, and then punish *us*. If Jesus suffered in my stead, I shall not suffer. If another has gone to prison and to death for me, I shall not go there. If the ax has fallen on the neck of Him that took my place, justice is satisfied, the law is vindicated, I am free, happy, joyful, grateful, and therefore bound forever to serve Him who loved me, and gave Himself for me.

I do not know how you look upon this doctrine, but it seems to me to be something worth telling everywhere. I would like to make every wind bear it on its wings, and every wave waft it on its crest. There is a just and righteous way to forgive sin, by Jesus bearing the death-penalty in the sinners' stead, that whosoever believes in Him, should be justified from all things, from which the law could not deliver him.

Now, these three things—that He poured out His soul unto death, and so bore the sinner's penalty; that He was numbered with the transgressors, and so stood side by side with sinners; and, next, that He actually bore their sin, and so came into a wonderful contact with sin, which did not defile Him, but which enabled Him to put away the sin which defiled men—these three things are the reasons of the glory of our Lord Jesus. God, for these three things, and one more, makes Him to divide the spoil with the strong, and divides Him a portion with the great.

He Made Intercession for the Transgressors

The last thing is this: HE MADE INTERCESSION FOR THE TRANSGRESSORS. You see all along, Christ gets His glory by standing side by side with guilty men. A curious mine it is to get gold out of. I will not venture to say what Augustine, in a burst of enthusiasm, once uttered. When speaking of Adam's fall, and then describing all the glory that comes to God out of the salvation of the guilty, that holy man could not help using the unguarded expression, "*Beata culpa!*" "Happy fault!" Yet, though I would not say so much as that, I do say that out of this dunghill of sin Christ has brought this diamond of His glory by our salvation. If there had been no sinners there could not have been a Savior. If no sin, no pouring out of the soul unto death; and if no pouring out of the soul unto death, no dividing a portion with the great. If there had been no guilt, there had been no act of expiation. In the wondrous act of expiation by our great Substitute, the Godhead is more gloriously revealed than in all the creations and providences of the divine power and wisdom.

> Sin, which stroke that love to quell,
>   Woke yet more its wondrous blaze;
> Eden, Bethlehem, Calvary, tell,
>   More than all beside, His praise.

In the person of His dying Son, bleeding for human guilt the Lord God has focused the splendor of His infinity. If you would see God, you must look to Calvary. God in Christ Jesus—this is God indeed. God in Christ Jesus bearing sin and putting it away—here you see what a God can do in boundless love. "God forbid that I should glory, save in the cross of our Lord Jesus Christ."

But this is the *finale* of it. He makes intercession for the transgressors. Who among us will take up the part of the guilty? Who will plead for the guilty? I know, in certain cases, the lawyer will sell his tongue to the most polluted; but if a man were perfectly pure, you would not find him saying a word in defense of the guilty; would you? So far as the man was guilty,

he could not be defended. Unless there were a fear of too severe a punishment, no one would take his part; and even in that case, the offender is
viewed as so far deserving that he is not guilty enough for so heavy a
penalty. For the guilty we could not plead, so as to deny or extenuate evil.
A just man would plead for innocent persons who might be falsely
accused; but our Lord made intercession *for transgressor's.*

When He was here on earth how tender He was with transgressors!
Women who were sinners came around Him, and He never bade them be
gone. She who was taken in adultery, O, how He dealt with her! When
Peter was about to deny Him, He said, "I have prayed for thee, that thy
faith fail not." Those nights out there on the cold mountains were not spent
for Himself, but for sinners. He bore on His heart the names of guilty men.
He was always pleading their cause, and when He came to die He said,
"Father, forgive them, for they know not what they do." He took their part,
you see. He would exculpate them if He could. I dare say that He has often
prayed like that for you. When you have been despising religion, and saying vile things about your Lord, He has said, "Ah, poor soul! It is like the
ravings of a man in a fever, who does not know what he is talking about.
He does not know what he is saying. Father, forgive him."

Our blessed Lord pleaded thus when He was here; and now He has
gone up yonder and is pleading still for the same persons. Though we cannot see through that veil which hides the invisible from us, yet the eye of
faith, I hope, is strong enough to see that He is at the Father's side at this
moment making intercession for transgressors. I do not picture Him up
yonder as using entreaties or pleading to an agony. O, no! With authority
He intercedes, for He has finished the work, and He claims the reward. I
do not even picture Him as using words. Those are the poor tools with
which men plead with men; but the death which our Lord endured for the
guilty is pleading with the Father. The death of Christ is a well-spring of
delight to God. The Father thinks of what Jesus has suffered in vindication
of the law, even of His obedience unto death; and that thought has power
with the Judge of all the earth. In effect, the wounds of Jesus perpetually
bleed. Still His cries of the great Sacrifice come up into His Father's ear.
The Godhead, delighted to bless, is charmed to find the way of blessing
men always open through the fact that the propitiation has been made, the
sin has been put away.

I cannot continue longer, for strength and time fail me. Only it does
seem to me so delightful to think that Jesus pleads *for sinners.* If you see
Him die, He is dying *for sinners.* If you see Him with His name written
down in a register, that register is the sinners' census book: His name is
written there that He may be in a position advantageous *for sinners.* If you
see Him pleading now that He is risen, He is the advocate *for sinners.* Did
you ever read this text in the Bible: "If any man does not sin, we have an

advocate with the Father, Jesus Christ the righteous"? No, you never did! But I will tell you what you do read there: "If any man sin, we have an advocate with the Father, Jesus Christ the righteous." "If any man sin." Is there anybody here that never sinned? Then there is no Christ for you. He never did anything for you, and never will. Are you guilty? Do you feel it? Do you confess it? Do you own it? Christ is for you.

If a doctor were to set up in the town, he would never think of sending out a circular in such terms as these: "Henry Smith, M.D.," invites healthy persons to call upon him, for he is proficient in the healing art." There will be no business for "Henry Smith, M.D.," among the healthy folks, let him be as learned as he may. And if he be known as an eminent physician, he does not need to intimate that sick persons are welcome to call upon him; for the very fact that he is a physician means that he seeks practice, and lives to serve the sick.

My Lord Jesus Christ, with all His saving power, cannot save those who do not need saving. It they have no sin, He cannot cleanse them from it. Can He? What, then, have some of you to do with the Savior? You are very good, respectable people, who have never done anything wrong in all your lives; what is Jesus to you? Of course, you go your own way, and take care of your own selves, and scout the idea of being beholden to free grace. Alas! this is folly. How foolish you are to think you are such characters! for you are nothing of the sort. If you look within, your heart is as foul as a black chimney that has never been swept. Our hearts are wells of defilement. O that you could see this, and quit your false righteousness! If you will not, there is nothing in Jesus for you. He derives His glory from sinners, not from self-conceited folks like you. But, you guilty ones, that will own and confess your guilt, may cheerfully remember that those four things which Jesus did, He did in connection with sinners, and it is because He did them in connection with sinners that He is this day crowned with glory and honor and majesty.

Jesus Christ does not shrink from sinners. What then? O you sinners, do not shrink from Him! If Jesus does not shrink from sinners—let me say it again—*you sinners, do not shrink from Him*. If we were to go today to some of those unhappy parts of the world in the north of Europe (it makes one's blood curdle to think that there are such places), where poor decaying lepers are made to live alone, and if these poor creatures came our way, we should wish them every blessing, and should desire for them every comfort; but while we were expressing our kind wishes, we should be gradually edging off, and leaving a distance between ourselves and their horrible pollution. That is not the way in which Jesus acts toward sinners: He draws near, and never sets a hedge between Himself and them. You need not undergo a quarantine before you may enter the port of salvation by Christ. Yonder is a filthy leprous sinner, as full of filth as an egg is full of meat, but Jesus comes right up to him, and lays His hand upon him, and says, "I will; be thou clean." Jesus never keeps at a distance from the sinner.

But suppose this poor leper began to run away from him. It would be natural that he should, but would also be very foolish. No, poor creature, stop running! Stay at Jesus' feet! Look to Him! Trust Him! Touch His garment and be healed! O my dear hearers, in this pulpit I seem to stand a long way off from you and talk to you from afar, but my heart is with you. I wish I knew how to persuade you to come to Jesus. I would use some loving logic, that I have not yet hit upon. How heartily would I entreat you to trust the Son of God, made flesh, bleeding and dying for guilty men! If you will trust Him, He will not deceive you, but you shall be saved, and saved at once and forever.

And, O you that love Him and know Him, will you learn one lesson, and then I will send you home? As Jesus does not shrink from sinners, *do not yourselves shrink from them.* You are not so pure and holy as He was, and yet He came into the world to save sinners. Go into the world to seek them. Be in earnest after sinners. You get so good, some of you, that there is no living with you. You forget the dunghills where you grew, and fancy yourselves angels, but you are nothing of the sort. God has made something of you, and now you are too respectable to look after those who are no worse than you were once.

If a man sins, you do not speak to him, lest you should be disgraced by his society. What pride! A man is known to be a drunkard, and there are some even of you who are teetotalers, who would not talk with such, but leave them till they are improved, and then you would speak to them. You will do them good if they come to you for it, but you will not go to them: you cannot bring your souls to handle the wound while it bleeds, and touch the filthy while they are foul.

Some are too fine and finicky to look after roughs. But I venture to say to the rough, the ragged, the graceless, the godless, that they are more likely to get a blessing than the self-righteous. I believe that there is more likelihood of converting a downright out-and-out sinner than of reaching the consciences of your very nice, neat, hypocritical people. Do not, therefore, shrink from sinners, for Jesus did not; and as from them He won His brightest trophies, even so may you. Be not ashamed, even if, by talking with sinners, you should come to be taken for one of them, for your Lord himself "was numbered with the transgressors; and he bare the sin of many, and made intercession for the transgressors." Let it be your vocation, as a man redeemed by blood, to be "the sinners' friend," henceforth and forever. God help you so to do!

O my beloved, may God send a blessing upon us at this hour. Pray for it. Pray for it. Lord, send it, for Jesus' sake! Amen.

12

*Christopathy**

With his stripes we are healed (Isaiah 53:5).

Brethren, whenever we come to talk about the passion of our Lord—and that subject is clearly brought before us here by the two words, "his stripes"—our feelings should be deeply solemn, and our attention intensely earnest. Put off your shoes from your feet when you draw near to this burning bush, for God is in it. If ever the spirit should be deeply penitential, and yet humbly confident, it ought to be so when we hear the lash falling upon the divine and human person of our blessed Master, and see Him wounded for our transgressions, and bruised for our iniquities.

Stand still, then, and see your Lord and Master fastened up to the Roman column, and cruelly scourged. Hear the terrible strokes, mark the bleeding wounds, and see how He becomes a mass of pain even as to His blessed body. Then note how His soul also is flagellated. Hark how the whips fall upon His spirit, till His inmost heart is wounded with the tortures, all but unbearable, which He endures for us. I charge my own heart to meditate upon this solemn theme without a single wandering thought, and I pray that you and I may be able to think together upon the matchless sufferings of Incarnate Love until our hearts melt within us in grateful love to Him.

Remember, brothers and sisters, that we were practically there when Jesus suffered those terrible stripes.

> Twas you, my sins, my cruel sins,
>   His chief tormentors were;
> Each of my crimes became a nail,
>   And unbelief the spear.

---

* This sermon was intended for reading on Sunday, January 10, 1897, at the Metropolitan Tabernacle, Newington, and was preached on Thursday evening, April 30, 1885, and is taken from *The Metropolitan Tabernacle Pulpit*.

We certainly had a share in His sorrows. O that we were equally certain that "with his stripes we are healed." You smote Him, dear friend, and you wounded Him; therefore, do not rest until you can say, "with his stripes I am healed." We must have a personal interest in this suffering One if we are to be healed by His stripes. We must get to lay our own hands upon this great sacrifice, and so accept it as being made on our behalf; for it would be a wretched thing to know that Christ was stricken, but not to know that "with his stripes we are healed." I would to God that not one should go out from this service without being able to say to himself as he retired, "Yes, blessed be His name, 'with his stripes I am healed.' The disease of sin is put away by the sacred balsam which drops from the side of the Crucified. From that mortal disease which else would surely have destroyed me, I am restored by His sufferings, His griefs, His death." And then, all together, may we be able to say, "with his stripes we are healed."

God Here Treats Sin as a Disease

Observe, dear friends, first of all, that GOD HERE TREATS SIN AS A DIS-EASE. There would be no need to talk about healing if sin had not been regarded by God as a disease. It is a great deal more than a disease, it is a willful crime; but still it is also a disease. It is often very difficult to separate the part in a crime which disease of the mind may have, and that portion which is distinctly willful. We need not make this separation ourselves. If we were to do so in order to excuse ourselves, that would only be increasing the evil; and if we do it for any other reason, we are so apt to be partial, that I am afraid we should ultimately make some kind of palliation for our sin which would not bear the test of the day of judgment. It is only because of God's sovereignty, and His infinite grace, and His strong resolve to have mercy upon men that, in this instance, He wills to look upon sin as a disease. He does not conceal from Himself, or from us, that it is a great and grievous fault; He calls it a trespass, a transgression, iniquity, and other terms that set forth its true character. Never in Scripture do we find any excuse for sin, or lessening of its heinousness; but in order that He might have mercy upon us, and deal graciously with us, the Lord is pleased to regard it as a disease, and then to come and treat us as a physician treats his patients, that He may cure us of the evil.

Sin is a disease, first, because *it is not an essential part of man as he was created.* It is something abnormal, it was not in human nature at the first. "God made man upright." Our first parent, as he came fresh from the hand of his Maker, was without taint or speck of sin; he had a healthy body inhabited by a healthy soul. There was about him no tendency to evil, he was created pure and perfect; and sin does not enter into the constitution of man, *per se*, as God made it. It is a something which has come into us from outside. Satan came with his temptation, and sin entered into us, and death by sin. Therefore, let no man, in any sense whatever, attribute sin to God as the Creator. Let him look upon sin as being a something extraneous to a man, something which ought never to have a *locus standi* within our nature at all, a something that is disturbing and destructive, a poisoned dart that is sticking in our flesh, abiding in our nature, and that has to be extracted by divine and sovereign grace.

And, secondly, sin is like a disease because *it puts all the faculties out of gear,* and breaks the equilibrium of the life forces, just as disease disturbs all our bodily functions. When a man is sick and ill, nothing about him works as it ought to do. There are some particular symptoms which, first of all, betray the existence of the *virus* of disease; but you cannot injure any one power of the body without the rest being in their measure put out of order. Thus has sin come into the soul of man, and put him altogether out of gear. Sometimes, a certain passion becomes predominant in a person quite out of proportion to the rest of his manhood. Things that might have been right in themselves, grow by indulgence into positive evils, while other things which ought to have had an open existence are suppressed until the suppression becomes a crime. It is sin that makes us wrong, and makes everything about us wrong, and makes us suffer we know not how much. The worst of the matter is that we do not ourselves readily perceive that we are the evil-doers, and we begin, perhaps, to judge others who are right, and because they are not precisely in the same condition as ourselves, we make our sinful selves to be the standard of equity, and consider that they are wrong, when all the while the evil is in ourselves. As long as a man is under the power of sin, his soul is under the power of a disease which has disturbed all his faculties, and taken away the correct action from every part of his being. Hence, God sees sin to be a disease, and we ought to thank Him that, in His gracious condescension, He deals with it in that way, instead of calling it what it really is, a crime deserving instant punishment.

Further, my friends, sin is a disease because it weakens the moral energy, just as many diseases weaken the sick person's body. A man, under the influence of some particular disease, becomes quite incapacitated for his ordinary work. There was a time when he was strong and athletic, but disease has entered his system, and so his nerves have lost their former force, and he, who would be the helper of others, becomes impotent, and needs to be waited upon himself. How often is a strong man brought down to utter helplessness! He who used to run like a hare must now be led out if he is to breathe the fresh air of heaven; he who once could cut with the ax, or smite with the hammer, must now be lifted and carried like a child.

You all know how greatly the body is weakened by disease, and just so is it with sin and the spirit. Sin takes away from the soul all power. Does not the apostle speak of us as being "without strength" when "in due time

Christ died for the ungodly"? The man has not the power or the will to believe in Christ, but yet he can believe a lie most readily, and he has no difficulty in cheating himself into self conceit. The man has not the strength to quit his sin, though he has power to pursue it with yet greater energy. He is weak in the knees, so that he cannot pray; he is weak in the eyes, so that he cannot see Jesus as his Savior; he is weak in the feet, so that he cannot draw near to God; he has withered hands, dumb lips, deaf ears, and he is palsied in his whole system. O sin, you take away from man the strength he needs with which to make the pilgrimage to heaven, or to go forth to war in the name of the Lord of hosts! Sin does all this, and yet men love it, and will not turn from it to Him who alone can destroy its deadly power.

I know that I am speaking to some who are well aware that sin has thrown their whole nature out of order, and taken away all their power to do that which is right. You, my friend, have come into this place, which is like the pool of Bethesda, with its five porches, and you have said in your heart, "O that the great Physician would come and heal me! I cannot step into the pool of His infinite mercy and love, though I would fain lie there waiting upon the means of grace; but I know that I shall find no benefit in the means of grace unless the Lord, who is the Giver of grace, shall come to me, and say, as He said to the man at the pool, 'Rise, take up thy bed, and walk.'" O what an awful mass of disease there is all round about us in these streets, and in these myriads of houses! Sin has done for mankind the most dreadful deeds; it is the direst of all calamities, the worst of all infections.

And, further, sin is like a disease because *it either causes great pain, or deadens all sensibility*, as the case may be; I do not know which one might rather choose, whether to be so diseased as to be full of pain, or to be suddenly smitten by a paralytic stroke, so as not to be able to feel at all. In spiritual things, the latter is the worse of the two evils. There are some sinners who appear to feel nothing; they sin, but their conscience does not accuse them concerning it. They purpose to go yet further into sin, and they reject Christ, and turn aside from Him even when the Spirit of God is striving with them, for they are insensible to the wrong they are doing. They do not feel, they cannot feel, and, alas! they do not even want to feel; they are callous and obdurate, and, as the apostle says, "past feeling." When they read or hear of the judgment to come, they do not tremble. When they are told about the love of Christ, they do not yield to Him. They can hear about His sufferings, and remain altogether unmoved; they have no fellowship with His sufferings, and scarcely know what the expression means. Sin is dear to them, even though it slew the Lord of glory Himself. This paralysis, this deadening of the powers is a very terrible phase of the disease of sin.

In some others, sin causes constant misery. I do not mean that godly sorrow which leads to penitence, for sin never brings its own repentance; but by way of remorse, or else of ungratified desire, or restlessness such as is natural to men who try to fill their immortal spirits with the empty joys of this poor world. Are there not many who, if they had all they have ever wished for, would still wish for more? If they could at this moment gratify every desire they have, they would but be as men who drink of the brine of the sea, whose thirst is not thereby quenched, but only increased. Believe me, you will never be content with the pleasures of this world, if your mind be at all aroused and awakened concerning your state in the sight of God! If you are given over to spiritual paralysis, you may be without feeling; but that is a deadly sign indeed.

But if there be any sort of spiritual life within you, the more you sin the more uneasy you will become. There is no way of peace by plunging more deeply into sin, as some think they will do—drowning dull care in the flowing bowl, or endeavoring to show their hardihood by rushing into still viler forms of lust, in order that they may, somehow or other, be satisfied and content. No, this disease breeds a hunger which increases as you feed it, it engenders a thirst which becomes the more intense the more you try to satisfy it.

Sin is also like a disease, because *it frequently produces a manifest pollution*. All disease in the body does pollute it in some way or other. Turn the microscope upon the part affected, and you will soon discover that there is something obnoxious there. But sin in the soul pollutes terribly in the sight of God. There are quiet, respectable sins which men can conceal from their fellow-creatures, so that they can keep their place in society, and seem to be all that they ought to be; but there are other sins which, like the leprosy of old, are white upon their brows. There are sins that are to be seen in the outward appearance of the man; his speech betrays him, his walk and conversation indicate what is going on within his heart. It is a dreadful thing for the sinner to recollect that he is a polluted being; until he is washed in Christ's precious blood, he is a being with whom God can have no sort of communion.

Men have to put infected persons away from the society of other people; under the Jewish law, when men were in a certain stage of disease, they had to be isolated altogether from their fellow-men, and certainly could not come into the house of the Lord. O my hearers, there are some of you who, if your bodies were as diseased as your souls are, would not dare even to show your faces in the streets; and some of us, who have been washed in the blood of Jesus, have felt ourselves to be so foul, so vile, so filthy, that if we could have ceased to exist we would have welcomed annihilation as a boon!

I remember the time when, under a sense of sin, I was afraid to pray. I did groan out a prayer of a sort; but I felt as if the very earth must be weary of bearing up such a sinner, and that the stars in their courses must be anxious to shoot baleful fires upon the one who was so defiled. Perhaps some of you have felt as I did, and now you join me in saying, "But we are washed, but we are sanctified, but we are justified in the name of the Lord Jesus, and by the Spirit of our God."

The disease that was upon us was worse than the foulest leprosy, more infectious than the most terrible fever, causing greater deformity than the dropsy, and working in us worse ills than the most foul disease that can ever fall upon the bodies of men. I would to God that men did but see that, although the picture I have tried to draw is terrible indeed, yet it is most gracious on God's part to treat them as diseased persons needing to be cured, rather than as criminals waiting to be executed.

Once more, sin is like disease because *it tends to increase in the man, and will one day prove fatal to him.* You cannot say to disease, "Hitherto shalt thou come, but no further." There are some diseases that seem to come very gradually, but they come very surely. There is the hectic flush, the trying cough, the painful breathing, and we begin to feel that consumption is coming; and very soon—terribly soon to those who love them—those who were once hale and hearty, to all appearance, become like walking skeletons, for the terrible disease has laid its cruel hand upon them, and will not let them go. So, my friend, as long as sin is in you, you need not deceive yourself, and think you can get rid of it when you will, for you cannot. It must be driven out by a higher power than your own; this disease must be cured by the great Physician, or else it will keep on increasing until at last you die. Sin will grow upon you till, "when it is finished, it bringeth forth death." God grant that, before that awful ending is reached, the Lord Jesus Christ may come and cure you, so that you may be able to say, "With his stripes we are healed."

Sin is a contagious disease, which passes from one to another. It is hereditary; it is universal; it is incurable; it is a mortal malady; it is a disease which no human physician can heal. Death, which ends all bodily pain, cannot cure this disease; it displays its utmost power in eternity, after the seal of perpetuity has been set upon it by the mandate, "He that is filthy, let him be filthy still." It is, in fact, such a disease that you were born with it, and you will bear it with you forever and ever, unless this wondrous prescription, of which we are now to speak, shall be accepted by you, and shall work in you the divine good pleasure, so that you shall be able to say, "With his stripes we are healed."

God Here Declares the Remedy Which He Has Provided

Now, secondly, we see from our text that GOD HERE DECLARES THE REMEDY WHICH HE HAS PROVIDED. Jesus Christ, His dear Son, has taken upon Himself our nature, and suffered on the cross in our stead, and God the Father has delivered Him up for us all, that we might be able to say, "With his stripes we are healed."

First, dear friends, *behold the heavenly medicine*—the stripes of Jesus in body and in soul. Picture Him before your mind's eye. He is scourged by the rough Roman soldiers till the sacred stream rolls down His back in a crimson tide, and He is scourged within as well as without till He cries, in utmost agony, "My God, my God, why hast thou forsaken me?" He is fastened to the cruel wood, His hands and feet and brow are all bleeding, and His inmost soul is poured out even unto death—whatever that wonderful expression may mean. He bears the sin of many, the chastisement of their peace is upon Him, He is bruised for their iniquities, and wounded for their transgressions. If you would be healed of sin's sickness, here is the medicine. Is it not singular surgery? Surgeons usually give us pain while trying to cure us, but here is a Physician who bears the pain Himself, and thereby heals us. Here is no medicine for us to take, for it has all been taken by Him. He suffers, He groans, He dies; and it is by His griefs and agonies that we are healed.

Then, next, *remember that the sufferings of Christ were vicarious.* He stood in our place that we might stand in His place. He took our sin upon Himself; and being found with that sin upon Him, He was made to bear the penalty that was due to it; and He did bear it, and this is the way whereby we are healed, by Jesus Christ Himself taking our infirmities, and bearing our sicknesses. This doctrine of substitution is the grandest of all truths, and though all these years I have continued to preach nothing else but this, what better news can I tell a poor sinner than that the Savior has taken his sins, and borne his sorrows for him?

Take away the doctrine of the substitutionary sacrifice of Christ, and you have torn out the very heart of the gospel. "The blood is the life thereof"; and you have no living gospel to preach if atonement by blood be once put into the background. But, O poor soul, if you believe that Jesus is the Christ, and that Christ took your sins, and bore them in His own body on the tree where He died, "the Just for the unjust, to bring us to God," you are saved, and saved forever!

This is how it is that "with his stripes we are healed." *Accept this atonement, and you are saved by it.* Does someone inquire, "How am I to get this atonement applied to my soul?" Well, first, the patient shows his wounds, and exhibits the progress of the disease; then, prayer begs for the divine surgery; next, belief in Christ is the linen cloth which binds on the plaister. If you believe on Jesus Christ, if you will accept the testimony of God concerning His Son whom He has set forth to be the propitiation for sin, and rely upon Him alone for salvation, you shall be saved. Faith, that is, trust, is the hand that brings the plaister to the wound, and holds it there till the blessed balsam has destroyed the venom that is within us. Trust yourself with Him who died for you, and you are saved; and continuing still to trust Him, you shall daily feel the power of His expiation, the marvelous healing that comes by His stripes. Repentance is the first symptom of that healing. When the proud flesh begins to yield, when the wretched gathering commences to break, and the soul that was formerly swollen through trying to conceal its sin bursts with confession and acknowledgment of its transgression, then is it being healed by the stripes of Jesus. This is God's wondrous remedy for the soul-sickness of sin.

But let me beg you to notice that *you must let nothing of your own interfere with this divine remedy*: "With his stripes we are healed." You see where prayer comes in; it does not heal, but it asks for the remedy. You see where trust comes in; it is not trust that heals, that is man's application of the great remedy. You see where repentance comes in; that is not what cures, it is a part of the cure, one of the first tokens that the blessed medicine has begun to work in the soul. "*With his stripes* we are healed." Will you notice that fact? The healing of a sinner does not lie in himself, nor in what he is, nor in what he feels, nor in what he does, nor in what he vows, nor in what he promises. It is not in himself at all; but there, at Gabbatha where the pavement is stained with the blood of the Son of God, and there, at Golgotha, where the place of a skull beholds the agonies of Christ. It is in His stripes that the healing lies.

I beseech you, do not scourge yourself: "With *his* stripes we are healed." I beg you, do not think that, by some kind of spiritual mortification, or terror, or horror, into which you are to force yourself, you shall be healed; your healing is in *His* stripes, not in your own; in *His* griefs, not in yours. Come away to Christ; and even if you are tempted to trust in your repentance, I implore you, do not make your repentance into a rival of the stripes of Jesus, for so it would become an anti-Christ. When your eyes are full of tears, look through them to Christ on the cross, for it is not a wet eye that will save you, but the Christ whom you may see, whether your eye be wet or dry. In the Christ upon the cross there are five wounds, but you have not to add even another one of your own to them. In him, and in Him alone, is all your healing; in Him who, from head to foot, becomes a mass of suffering, that you, diseased from head to foot, might from the crown of your head to the sole of your foot be made perfectly whole.

The Divine Remedy Is Immediately Effective

Now I must close with the third reflection, which is this—THE DIVINE REMEDY IS IMMEDIATELY EFFECTIVE. "With his stripes we are healed." To the carnal mind, it does not seem as if the sufferings of Christ could touch the case at all; but those who have believed in the stripes of Jesus are witnesses to the instant and perfect efficacy of the medicine. We can many of us speak from experience, since we can say that "we are healed." How are we healed?

Well, first, *our conscience is healed of every smart*. God is satisfied with Christ, and so are we. If, for Christ's sake, He has put away sin without dishonor to Himself, then are we also perfectly content and full of rejoicing in the atonement, and we need nothing else to keep our conscience quiet.

By these same wounds of Christ *our heart is healed of its love of sin.* It was once in love with sin, but now it hates all iniquity. If our Redeemer died because of our sin, how can we live any longer therein? All our past thoughts concerning sin are turned upside down or reversed. Sin gave us pleasure once, but now it gives us the utmost pain, and we desire to be free from it, and to be perfectly holy; there is no evil that we would harbor in our bosoms. It did seem a singular thing that we should look to Christ, and so find pardon, and that at that same moment we should be totally changed in our nature as to our view of sin, yet it did so happen. While sin was on us, we felt as if we had no hope, and therefore we went on in sin; but when sin was pardoned, then we felt great joy, and consequent gratitude and love to God. A sinner repents of his sins much more after they are pardoned than he does before, and so he sings—

> I know they are forgiven,
> But still their pain to me
> Is all the grief and anguish
> They laid, my Lord, on Thee.

Our cry is, "Death to sin, now that Christ has died for sin!" "If the One died for all, then all died"; and as in Christ we died to sin, how shall we live any longer therein? You may preach mere morality till there shall be no morality left; but preach the atoning sacrifice of Christ, and the pardoning love of the Father, and then the immoral will be changed, and follow after holiness with a greater eagerness than ever possessed them while they followed after sin.

By this divine remedy *our life is healed of its rebellion.* This medicine has worked within the heart, and it has also worked without in the life. Now has the drunkard become sober, and he hates the cup he used to love. Now has the swearer's foul mouth been washed, and his lips, once so polluted, are like lilies dropping sweet-smelling myrrh. Now has the cruel and unkind one become tender, gentle, and loving, the false has become true, the proud bends his neck in humility, the idle has become a diligent servant of Christ; the transformation is wonderful, and this is the secret, "With his stripes we are healed."

Yet once more, *our consciousness assures us that we are healed.* We know that we are healed, and we rejoice in the fact, and we are not to be disputed out of it. There seems to be a theory, held by some people, to the effect that we cannot tell whether we are saved or not. When we have had a disease in our body, we can tell whether we have been healed or not; and the marks and evidences of the supernatural change that takes place within the spirit are as apparent, as a usual rule, and certainly as positive and sure, as the changes wrought in the body by healing medicine. We know that we are healed. I am not talking to you of a thing which I do not know personally for myself. When the text says, "We," my heart says, "I," and I am longing that everybody here should be able to put his own seal to it, and say, "That is true; with *his* stripes we are healed, with his stripes *we* are healed, with his stripes we *are* healed." I will not go into the stories of some who are here—stories that I know of the marvelous change that grace has made in your characters and lives; but you can bear witness, as can all the saints in heaven, that "with His stripes we are healed."

My last word is that, if you are healed by His stripes, you should go and live like healthy men. When a man is healed of disease, he does not continue to lie in bed; so, dear friends, do not any of you be lazy Christians. When a man is healed, he does not sit down and groan about the disease that is gone; so do not you be continually groaning and croaking and sighing. When a man is healed, he likes to go and tell about the remedy to others; so, dear friends, do not keep to yourselves the news of this blessed heavenly balsam, but go and tell the tidings everywhere, "With his stripes we are healed." When a man is healed, he is joyful, and begins to sing with gladness; so, go and sing, and praise and bless the Lord all your days.

When Christ heals, you know, people do not get the sickness back again. His cures are cures for life, and cures for eternity. If the devil goes out of a man of his own accord, he always comes back again, and brings seven others with him; but, if Christ turns him out, I promise you that he will never be allowed to come back again. When the strong Man armed has dislodged the devil, He keeps the house that He has won, and takes good care that, neither by the front door nor by the back, shall the old enemy ever come back again. Having by His own right hand and His holy arm gotten the victory, He challenges the foeman to take back His spoil, crying, "shall the prey be taken from the mighty, or the lawful captive delivered?" No; that shall never be, so you may go on your way rejoicing, and sing as you go, "With his stripes we are healed." This is not a temporary remedy; it is a medicine which, when it once gets into the soul, breeds therein health that shall make that soul perfectly whole, so that at last, among the holy ones before the throne of God on high, that man shall sing with all his fellows, "'With his stripes we are healed.' Glory be to the bleeding Christ! All honor, and majesty, and dominion, and praise be unto him forever, and ever!" And let all the healed ones say, "Amen, and Amen."

13
Cries from the Cross[*]

My God, my God, why hast thou forsaken me? why art thou so far from helping me, and from the words of my roaring? (Psalm 22:1).

We here behold the Savior in the depths of His agonies and sorrows. No other place so well shows the griefs of Christ as Calvary, and no other moment at Calvary is so full of agony as that in which this cry rends the air, "My God, my God, why hast thou forsaken me!" At this moment, physical weakness, brought upon Him by fasting and scourging, was united with the acute mental torture which He endured from the shame and ignominy through which He had to pass; and as the culmination of His grief, He suffered spiritual agony which surpasses all expression, on account of the departure of His Father from Him. This was the blackness and darkness of His horror; then it was that He penetrated the depths of the caverns of suffering.

"My God, my God, why hast thou forsaken me?" There is something in these words of our Savior always calculated to benefit us. When we behold the sufferings of men, they afflict and appall us; but the sufferings of our Savior, while they move us to grief, have about them something sweet, and full of consolation. Here, even here, in this black spot of grief, we find our heaven, while gazing upon the cross. This, which might be thought a frightful sight, makes the Christian glad and joyous. If he laments the cause, yet he rejoices in the consequences.

---

[*] This sermon was intended for reading on Sunday, March 27, 1898, at New Park Street Chapel, Southwark, and was preached on Sunday evening, November 2, 1856. It is taken from *The Metropolitan Tabernacle Pulpit*. This was the first sermon preached by Mr. Spurgeon after the fatal calamity at the Surrey Gardens Music Hall, a fortnight previously. On commencing his discourse, he said, "The observations I have to make will be very brief, seeing that afterward we are to partake of the Lord's supper. I shall make no allusion to the recent catastrophe. I hope, however, to improve that event at some future period."

Three Questions

First, in our text, there are THREE QUESTIONS to which I shall call your attention.

The first is, *"My God my God, why hast thou forsaken me?"* By these words we are to understand that our blessed Lord and Savior was at that moment forsaken by God in such a manner as He had never been before. He had battled with the enemy in the desert, but thrice He overcame him, and cast him to the earth. He had striven with that foe all His life long, and even in the garden He had wrestled with him till His soul was "exceeding sorrowful." It is not till now that He experiences a depth of sorrow which He never felt before. It was necessary that He should suffer, in the stead of sinners, just what sinners ought to have suffered. It would be difficult to conceive of punishment for sin apart from the frown of Deity. With crime we always associate anger, so that, when Christ died, "the Just for the unjust, that he might bring us to God"—when our blessed Savior became our Substitute, He became, for the time, the victim of His Father's righteous wrath, seeing that our sins had been imputed to Him, in order that His righteousness might be imputed to us. It was necessary that He should feel the loss of His Father's smile—for the condemned in hell must have tasted of that bitterness; and therefore the Father closed the eye of His love, put the hand of justice before the smile of His face, and left His Son to cry, "My God, my God, why hast thou forsaken me?"

There is no man living who can tell the full meaning of these words; not one in heaven or on earth—I had almost said, in hell; there is not a man who can spell these words out with all their depth of misery. Some of us think, at times, that *we* could cry, "My God, my God, why hast thou forsaken me?" There are seasons when the brightness of our Father's smile is eclipsed by clouds and darkness. But let us remember that God never does really forsake us. It is only a seeming forsaking with us, but in Christ's case it was a real forsaking. God only knows how much we grieve, sometimes, at a little withdrawal of our Father's love; but the real turning away of God's face from His Son—who shall calculate how deep the agony which it caused Him when He cried, "My God, my God, why hast thou forsaken me?"

In our case, this is the cry of unbelief; in His case, it was the utterance of a fact, for Cod had really turned away from Him for a time. "O poor, distressed soul, who once lived in the sunshine of God's face, but is now in darkness—you who are walking in the valley of the shadow of death, you hear noises, and you are afraid; your soul is startled within you, you are stricken with terror if you think that God has forsaken you! Remember that He has not real forsaken you, for—

> Mountains when in darkness shrouded,
> Are as real as in day.

God in the clouds is as much our God as when He shines forth in all the luster of His benevolence; but since even the *thought* that He has forsaken us gives us agony, what must the agony of the Savior have been when He cried, "My God, my God, why hast thou forsaken me?"

The next question is, *"Why art thou so far from helping me?"* Hitherto, God had helped His Son, but now He must tread the wine press alone, and even His own Father cannot be with Him. Have you not felt, sometimes, that God has brought you to do some duty, and yet has apparently not given you the strength to do it? Have you never felt that sadness of heart which makes you cry, "Why art thou so far from helping me?" But if God means you to do anything, you can do it, for He will give you the power. Perhaps your brain reels; but God has ordained that you must do it, and you shall do it. Have you not felt as if you must go on even while, every step you took, you were afraid to put your foot down for fear you should not get a firm foothold? If you have had any experience of divine things, it must have been so with you. We can scarcely guess what it was that our Savior felt when He said, "Why art thou so far from helping me?" His work is one which none but a Divine Person could have accomplished, yet His Father's eye was turned away from Him! With more than Herculean labors before Him, but with none of His Father's might given to Him, what must have been the strain upon Him! Truly, as Hart says, He—

> Bore all incarnate God could bear,
> With strength enough, and none to spare.

The third inquiry is, *"Why art thou so far from the words of my roaring?"* The word here translated "roaring" means, in the original Hebrew, that deep, solemn groan which is caused by serious sickness, and which suffering men utter. Christ compares His prayers to those roarings, and complains that God is so far from Him that He does not hear Him. Beloved, many of us can sympathize with Christ here. How often have we on our knees asked some favor of God, and we thought we asked in faith, yet it never came! Down we went upon our knees again. There is something which withholds the answer; and, with tears in our eyes, we have wrestled with God again; we have pleaded, for Jesus' sake, but the heavens have seemed like brass. In the bitterness of our spirit, we have cried, "Can there *be* a God?" And we have turned round, and said, "'My God, my God, why hast thou forsaken me? Why art thou so far from the words of my roaring?' Is this like you? Dost you ever spurn a sinner? Have you not said, 'Knock, and it shall be opened unto thee?' Are you reluctant to be kind? Do you withhold your promise?" And when we have been almost ready to give up, with everything apparently against us, have we not *groaned*, and said, "Why art thou so far from the words of my roaring?" Though we know something, it is not much that we can truly understand of those direful sorrows and agonies which our blessed Lord endured when He asked these three questions, "My God, my God, why hast thou forsaken me? why art thou so far from helping me, and from the words of my roaring?"

Look at the Answers to These Three Questions

Let us now, in the second place, LOOK AT THE ANSWERS TO THESE THREE QUESTIONS. The answer to the first question I have given before. I think I hear the Father say to Christ, "*My Son I forsake thee because thou standest in the sinner's stead.* As thou art holy, just, and true, I never would forsake *thee*; I would never turn away from *thee*; for, even as a man, thou hast been holy, harmless, undefiled, and separate from sinners; but on thy head doth rest the guilt of every penitent, transferred from him to thee; and thou must expiate it by thy blood. Because thou standest in the sinner's stead, I will not look at thee till thou hast borne the full weight of my vengeance. *Then*, I will exalt thee on high, far above all principalities and powers."

O Christian, pause here, and reflect! Christ was punished in this way for you! O see that countenance so wrung with horror; those horrors gather there for you! Perhaps, in your own esteem, you are the most worthless of the family; certainly, the cost insignificant; but the meanest lamb of Christ's flock is as much the object of purchase as any other. Yes, when that black darkness gathered round His brow, and when He cried out, "Eloi, Eloi," in the words of our text, for the Lord Omnipotent to help Him; when He uttered that awfully solemn cry, it was because He loved you, because He gave Himself for you, that you might be sanctified here, and dwell with Him hereafter. God forsook Him, therefore, first, because He was the sinner's Substitute.

The answer to the second question is, "*Because I would have thee get all the honor to thyself*; therefore I will not help thee, lest I should have to divide the spoil with thee." The Lord Jesus Christ lived to glorify His Father, and He died to glorify Himself, in the redemption of His chosen people. God says, "No, My Son, you shall do it alone; for You must wear the crown alone; and upon Your person shall all the regalia of your sovereignty be found. I will give you all the praise, and therefore you shall accomplish all the labor." He was to tread the wine-press alone, and to get the victory and glory alone to Himself.

The answer to the third question is essentially the same as the answer to the first. *To have heard Christ's prayer at that time would hate been inappropriate.* This turning away of the Divine Father from hearing His

Son's prayer is just in keeping with His condition; as the sinner's Surety, His prayer must not be heard; as the sinner's Surety, He could say, "Now that I am here, dying in the sinner's stead, you seal your ears against My prayer." God did not hear His Son, because He knew His Son was dying to bring us near to God, and the Son therefore cried, "My God, my God, why hast thou forsaken me?''

A Word of Earnest Exhortation and Affectionate Warning

In conclusion, I shall offer you A WORD OF EARNEST EXHORTATION AND AFFECTIONATE WARNING. Is it nothing to some of you that Jesus should die? You hear the tale of Calvary; but, alas! you have dry eyes. You never weep concerning it. Is the death of Jesus nothing to you? Alas! it seems to be so with many. Your hearts have never throbbed in sympathy with Him. O friends, how many of you can look on Christ, thus agonizing and groaning, and say, "He is *my* Ransom, *my* Redeemer"? Could you say, with Christ, "*My* God"? Or is God another's, and not yours? O if you are out of Christ, hear me speak one word, it is a word of *warning*! Remember, *to be out of Christ, is to be without hope*; if you die unsprinkled with His blood, you are lost. *And what is it to be lost*? I shall not try to tell you the meaning of that dreadful word "*lost.*" Some of you may know it before another sun has risen. God grant that you may not!

Do you desire to know how you may be saved? Hear me. "God so loved the world, that he gave his only begotten Son, that whosoever believeth in him should not perish, but have everlasting life." "He that believeth and is baptized shall be saved." To be baptized is to be buried in water in the name of the Father, and of the Son, and of the Holy Spirit. Have you believed in Christ? Have you professed faith in Christ? Faith is the grace which rests alone on Christ.

Whosoever will be saved, before all things it is necessary that he should feel himself to be lost—that he should know himself to be a ruined sinner, and then he should believe this: "It is a faithful saying, and worthy of all acceptation, that Christ Jesus came into the world to save sinners," even the very chief. You want no mediator between yourselves and Christ. You may come to Christ just as you are—guilty, wicked, poor; just as you are, Christ will take you. There is no necessity for washing beforehand. You want no riches; in Him you have *all* you require, will you bring anything to "*all*"? You want no garments; for in Christ you have a seamless robe which will amply suffice to cover even the biggest sinner upon earth, as well as the least.

Come, then, to Jesus at once. Do you say you do not know *how* to come? Come just as you are. Do not wait to *do* anything. What you want is to leave off doing, and let Christ do all for you. What do you want to do, when He has done all? All the labor of your hands can never fulfill what God commands. Christ died for sinners, and you must say, "Sink or swim, I will have no other Savior but Christ." Cast yourself wholly upon Him.

> And when thine eye of faith is dim,
> Still trust in Jesus, sink or swim;
> Still at His footstool humbly bow
> O sinner! sinner! *prostrate now!*

He is able to pardon you at this moment. There are some of you who know you are guilty, and groan concerning it. Sinner, why do you tarry? "Come, and welcome!" is my Master's message to you. If you feel you are lost and ruined, there is not a barrier between you and heaven; Christ has broken it down.

If you know of your own lost estate, Christ has died for you; believe, and come! Come, and welcome, sinner, come! O sinner, come! Come! Come! Jesus bids you come; and as His ambassador to you, I bid you come, as One who would *die* to save your souls if it were necessary—as One who knows how to groan over you, and to weep over you—One who loves you even as He loves Himself—I, as His minister, say to you, in God's name, and in Christ's stead, "Be reconciled to God." What say you? Has God made you willing? Then rejoice! Rejoice, for He has not made you willing without giving you the power to do what He has made you willing to do. Come! Come! This moment you may be as sure of heaven as if you were there, if you cast yourself upon Christ, and have nothing but Jesus for your soul's reliance.